500 Tips on Assessment

There is an increasing pressure on teachers in further and higher education to provide assessment systems that are fair, valid, reliable, efficient and effective. Funding bodies demand higher quality, students themselves have sharpening expectations. Traditionally, assessment of students' work has caused teachers more difficulties than any other area, yet the growing number of students and severe financial restraints mean that even existing standards are difficult to maintain.

In this completely updated edition of *500 Tips on Assessment*, the authors look at the questions and the problems that teachers face and provide them with practical guidance. Their advice is down-to-earth, jargon free and digestible, covering such key issues as:

- Putting assessment into context – best practice, learning outcomes and monitoring quality of assessment
- Different examination formats – traditional, open-book, open-notes, oral exams
- Different assessment formats – essays, reports, practical work, presentations
- Feedback and assessment
- Assessing group learning

500 Tips on Assessment is an invaluable dip-in aid for hard-pressed lecturers and teachers in further and higher education. It should be read, enjoyed and seriously considered by all those concerned about the quality and appropriateness of their assessment methods.

Professor Phil Race works part-time at the University of Leeds, and is a staff development consultant in further and higher education for the rest of his time. **Professor Sally Brown** is Visiting Professor of Learning and Teaching at the Leeds Metropolitan University, and also at the Robert Gordon University in Aberdeen and Buckingham Chilterns University College. She is also an independent higher education consultant, change manager and interim manager. **Professor Brenda Smith** is Head of the Generic Centre of the Higher Education Academy, and has facilitated workshops and seminars extensively internationally.

New Editions in the 500 Tips Series

500 Tips for Open and Online Learning, 2nd edition
Phil Race

500 Tips for Tutors, 2nd edition
Phil Race and Sally Brown

500 Tips on Assessment, 2nd edition
Phil Race, Sally Brown and Brenda Smith

500 Tips on Assessment

Second edition

Phil Race, Sally Brown and Brenda Smith

 RoutledgeFalmer
Taylor & Francis Group

LONDON AND NEW YORK

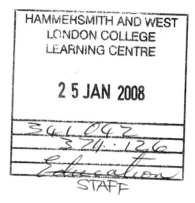

First edition published in 1996 by Kogan Page Ltd
Reprinted in 2000, 2002 by Kogan Page Ltd

This edition published 2005 by RoutledgeFalmer
2 Park Square, Milton Park, Abingdon, Oxon, OX14 4RN

Simultaneously published in the USA and Canada
by RoutledgeFalmer
270 Madison Ave, New York, NY 100016

RoutledgeFalmer is an imprint of the Taylor & Francis Group

© 2005 Phil Race, Sally Brown and Brenda Smith

Typeset in Garamond by Keystroke, Jacaranda Lodge, Wolverhampton
Printed and bound in Great Britain by MPG Books Ltd, Bodmin

British Library Cataloguing in Publication Data
A catalogue record for this book is available from the British Library

Library of Congress Cataloging in Publication Data
A catalog record for this book has been requested

ISBN 0–415–34279–1

Contents

List of illustrations   vii
Preface to the second edition   ix

Chapter 1   Putting assessment into context   **1**
  1   Values for best practice in assessment   2
  2   Why should we assess?   5
  3   What are we assessing? A checklist   8
  4   When should we assess?   10
  5   Designing learning outcomes and linking them to assessment   12
  6   Plagiarism, cheating and assessment   16
  7   Monitoring the quality of assessment processes   18
  8   Don't assess like this!   21
  9   'I wish I hadn't done that!'   23

Chapter 2   Exams of various sorts   **26**
 10   Traditional unseen, time-constrained written exams   27
 11   Open-book exams   40
 12   Open-notes exams   42
 13   Structured exams   44
 14   Vivas – oral exams   49
 15   Some other kinds of examination   53

Chapter 3   Specific assessment formats   **55**
 16   Essays   56
 17   Reviews and annotated bibliographies   60
 18   Reports   64
 19   Practical work   68
 20   Portfolios   71
 21   Presentations   78
 22   Assessing performances   86

23 Student projects   89
24 Poster displays and exhibitions   93
25 Dissertations and theses   97
26 Work-based learning   100

Chapter 4 Feedback and assessment   **104**
27 Quality of feedback   105
28 Helping students to make the most of your feedback   107
29 Reducing your load: short cuts to good feedback   110
30 Feedback in writing or print   113
31 Face-to-face feedback   119
32 Electronic feedback   122

Chapter 5 Involving students in their own assessment   **130**
33 Why consider student peer assessment?   131
34 What lends itself to peer assessment?   133
35 Getting started with peer assessment   135
36 Getting students to formulate criteria   137
37 Student self-assessment   144
38 Setting up self-assessment tutor dialogues   147
39 Further questions to elicit reflection   150
40 Yet more questions to promote reflection   153

Chapter 6 Assessing group learning   **156**
41 Take the simplest path   157
42 Divide and concur   158
43 Add differentials   159
44 Add contribution marks   161
45 Add more tasks   162
46 Test them orally   163
47 Test them in writing   164

References and further reading   165

Index   168

Illustrations

Figures

1   Linking learning outcomes, evidence of achievement, assessment criteria and feedback   13
2   Portfolio assessment form   76
3   Peer assessment grid   142
4   Peer assessment with feedback   143

Tables

1   Advantages and disadvantages of assessment via traditional time-constrained unseen written exams   27
2   Task: what do you think traditional exams really measure?   34
3   Advantages and disadvantages of assessment via open-book exams   40
4   Advantages and disadvantages of assessment via open-notes exams   42
5   Advantages and disadvantages of assessment via structured exams   44
6   Advantages and disadvantages of assessment via vivas   49
7   Advantages and disadvantages of assessment via essay examination questions   56
8   Advantages and disadvantages of assessment via student-produced annotated bibliographies   60
9   Advantages and disadvantages of assessment via students' reports   64
10   Advantages and disadvantages of assessment via practical work   68
11   Advantages and disadvantages of assessment via students' portfolios   71
12   Advantages and disadvantages of assessment via student's presentations   78
13   Case-study group presentations competition: your criticisms, and suggestions for improvement   83
14   Case-study group presentations competition: our criticisms, and suggestions for improvement   84
15   Advantages and disadvantages of assessment via student performances   86

16   Advantages and disadvantages of assessment via project work   89
17   Advantages and disadvantages of assessment via poster displays
     and exhibitions   93
18   Advantages and disadvantages of assessment via dissertations and
     theses   97
19   Advantages and disadvantages of assessment via work-based learning   100
20   Advantages and disadvantages of feedback presented via
     handwritten comments   113
21   Advantages and disadvantages of feedback presented via
     word-processed comments   114
22   Advantages and disadvantages of feedback presented via model
     answers or solutions   115
23   Advantages and disadvantages of feedback presented via
     assignment return sheets   115
24   Advantages and disadvantages of feedback presented via
     word-processed overall class reports   116
25   Advantages and disadvantages of feedback presented via codes
     written on students' work   117
26   Advantages and disadvantages of face-to-face feedback to whole
     classes   119
27   Advantages and disadvantages of face-to-face feedback to
     individual students   120
28   Advantages and disadvantages of face-to-face feedback to small
     groups of students   121
29   Advantages and disadvantages of feedback presented via emailed
     comments on students' assessed work   122
30   Advantages and disadvantages of feedback presented via computer
     conferences   123
31   Advantages and disadvantages of computer-delivered feedback   124
32   Group learning: advantages and disadvantages of giving all group
     members the same mark   157
33   Group learning: advantages and disadvantages of dividing up the
     group task and assessing each component separately   158
34   Group learning: advantages and disadvantages of negotiating
     differentials between group members   159
35   Group learning: advantages and disadvantages of having group
     members peer-assess individual members' contribution   161
36   Group learning: advantages and disadvantages of adding
     individual assessed tasks   162
37   Group learning: advantages and disadvantages of testing group
     members orally   163
38   Group learning: advantages and disadvantages of testing group
     members in writing   164

Preface to the second edition

In the eight years since we wrote the first edition of this book, much has changed in higher education. These years have seen major developments in quality assurance, and codes of practice have been published in the United Kingdom by the Quality Assurance Agency for Higher Education (QAA), the most relevant relating directly to assessment. The Quality and Curriculum Agency (QCA) has similarly tightened up assessment processes and practices in vocational and further education. Higher education institutions in the United Kingdom have developed strategies on teaching and learning (including assessment) for the funding bodies.

Furthermore, new legislation in the United Kingdom has repealed the 'education exemption' that formerly existed in the applicability of the 1995 Disability Discrimination Act, and since 2002 the need to comply with the Special Educational Needs and Disabilities Act (SENDA) has caused most staff in tertiary education to revisit and improve assessment practices, processes and instruments.

Accordingly, many of the suggestions we made in the first edition have been further developed since 1996, for example in *2000 Tips for Lecturers* (1999) and the second edition of *The Lecturer's Toolkit* (2001). It is therefore these later versions of our ideas that form the basis of this second edition of the present book, to which we have added various new suggestions and some illustrative case-study material.

There is no escaping from the conclusion that we have all become much more accountable for the assessment dimensions of our work. We have not written specific sections of this book, however, to address compliance with SENDA or the QAA Codes of Practice or the QCA agenda. Good assessment practice, as we suggest throughout this book, automatically ensures that assessment is as inclusive as we can make it (to meet the SENDA agenda) and is valid, reliable, transparent and authentic (to meet the QAA and QCA agendas). Inclusive assessment is *good* assessment; what works well for students with special needs works just as well for students without any special needs – not least, clearly worded, unambiguous assessment questions or task briefings.

Current thinking now aims to ensure that assessment practices and procedures are constructively aligned (Biggs, 2003) with the learning outcomes we set for our students, requiring a more systematic approach to assessment design.

Students themselves are changing, too. They are increasingly strategic – an intelligent and understandable reaction to the situation they find themselves in when participating in post-compulsory education. Assessment is more than ever the driving force for their learning. Students may wish to be regarded as customers or clients, and they are more forthcoming in their views of their learning experience, more aware of their rights, and more willing to challenge their tutors or examiners or institutions if they think they are not being treated fairly. They are more litigious – as is most of society around them. They are on the whole much more computer literate – and for many, this means they may be less comfortable and less confident when being assessed on the basis of what they write with pen and paper, than on what they produce with keyboard, mouse and the Internet.

Furthermore, students have increased in numbers. There are many more of them in our lecture theatres, classrooms, and examinations halls. Widening participation targets in England are presently set at around 50 per cent participation in higher education of the 18–30 age group, as opposed to around 5 per cent when we ourselves were students – a very different learning climate. An increased proportion of students enter university without having a family history of participation in higher education, and have no close relatives or friends to alert them to how it all works in practice. There is a much greater range of ability in most large classes now – and this is of course reflected in the data that assessment yields. A significantly greater proportion of students now need focused help on how best to prepare themselves for the different assessment processes and instruments that they will meet on their journey towards the qualifications they seek.

For this edition we have divided the content of the book into six chapters. Chapter 1 now contains our thinking on assessment in general, with an expanded review of the design and use of learning outcomes, and we have gone into considerably more detail about various kinds of examination formats in Chapter 2. Chapter 3 presents suggestions about a range of specific assessment formats, and we have extended our discussion of feedback in Chapter 4, and our coverage of self-assessment and peer assessment in Chapter 5. We have also included a discussion on assessing group learning as Chapter 6.

To make room for the new content, we have had to miss out from this edition some of the topics covered by its predecessor. For example, we don't at present include suggestions for external examiners, not least because in the United Kingdom this area is about to be the focus of a great deal of development arising from the Government White Paper published in January 2003, leading towards the development of systematic training and support for people undertaking this role. This process is due to be overseen by the newly formed Higher Education Academy, inaugurated in 2004 from a merger of the Institute for Learning and Teaching in Higher Education, the Learning and Teaching Support Networks and the National Coordination Team.

In various parts of the book we now include 'advantages' and 'disadvantages' relating to various assessment and feedback processes, to help you to decide which are fit for purpose in your own context, and to add perspective to our suggestions about how best to make assessment and feedback work in general. We have also added some illustrative material to bring to life some of the more important issues we have addressed.

How we assess our students has a profound effect both on what they learn, and on the ways in which they learn. If our choices of assessment strategies provide students with systems under which they are goaded into activities that privilege short-term memory, information recall and surface learning, then we should not be surprised if the outcomes are poor in terms of learning pay-off. There is no getting away from the fact that most of the things that go wrong with assessment are our fault, the result of poor assessment design – and not the fault of our students.

In this book we aim to provide hard-pressed lecturers in higher and further education with practical guidance on how to tackle the key issues in assessment. This should not be seen as a recipe book on how to get assessment right, but rather as a starting point providing ideas from which you can choose those that may be most suitable for your own particular students, in the specific discipline or environment you work in.

A final reminder: nothing that we do to, or for, our students is more important than our assessment of their work and the feedback we give them on it. The results of our assessment influence our students for the rest of their lives and careers – fine if we get it right, but unthinkable when we get it wrong. We must therefore all strive to make every element of assessment in which we are involved as valid as we can, as reliable as we can and as transparent as we can. We simply aim in this book to help you to do this for your students.

Phil Race, Sally Brown and Brenda Smith
April 2004

Chapter 1

Putting assessment into context

1   Values for best practice in assessment
2   Why should we assess?
3   What are we assessing? A checklist
4   When should we assess?
5   Designing learning outcomes and linking them to assessment
6   Plagiarism, cheating and assessment
7   Monitoring the quality of assessment processes
8   Don't assess like this!
9   'I wish I hadn't done that!'

1

Values for best practice in assessment

We begin this book by identifying some values as a starting point on our mission to optimise assessment in terms of validity, reliability, authenticity and transparency. For a start, let's try to define or explain these terms in straightforward English, and add some further values to work towards in our assessment. We have continued to address the agenda in this section throughout the book, so please regard this initial exposition as just a summary of the overall picture.

1   **Assessment should be valid.** It should assess what it is that you really want to measure. For example, when you are attempting to assess problem-solving skills, the assessment should be dependent not on the quality and style of the production of written reports on problem-solving, but on the quality of the solutions devised.

2   **Assessment should be reliable.** If we can get the task briefings, assessment criteria and marking schemes right, there should be good inter-assessor reliability (when more than one assessor marks the work), as well as good intra-assessor reliability (assessors should come up with the same results when marking the same work on different occasions). All assignments in a batch should be marked to the same standard. (This isn't the same as the strange notion of benchmarking, which implies that assignments should hit the same standards in every comparable course in existence – an interesting but quite unachievable idea.)

3   **Assessment should be transparent.** There should be no hidden agendas. There should be no nasty surprises for students. Students should not be playing the game 'guess what's in our assessors' minds'. Assessment should be in line with the intended learning outcomes as published in student handbooks and syllabus documentation, and the links between these outcomes and the assessment criteria we use should be plain to see (not just by external scrutineers such as QAA reviewers, but by students themselves).

4   **Assessment should be authentic.** There are at least two dimensions to this. First, we need to be striving to measure each student's achievement, in ways that enable us to be certain that the achievement belongs to the student and not to anyone else. Second, we need to be measuring students' achievement of the intended outcomes in contexts that are as close as possible to the intentions lying behind the outcomes in the first place – for example, performance skills should be measured in performances, not just where students are writing about performance in exam rooms.

5   **Assessment should motivate students to learn.** Assessment should help them to structure their learning continuously during their studies, not just in a few critical weeks before particular assessment climaxes. Assessment should allow students to self-assess and monitor their progress throughout a course, and help them to make informed choices about what to learn, how to learn it, and how best to evidence the achievement of their learning.

6   **Assessment should promote deep learning.** Students should not be driven towards surface or 'reproductive' learning because of the ways their learning is to be assessed. They should not find themselves 'clearing their minds of the last subject in order to make room for the next subject'.

7   **Assessment should be fair.** Students should have equivalence of opportunities to succeed even if their experiences are not identical. This is particularly important when we are assessing work based in individual learning contracts. It is also important that all assessment instruments and processes should be *seen to be fair* by all students.

8   **Assessment should be equitable.** While assessment overall may be designed to discriminate between students on the basis of the extent to which they have achieved the intended learning outcomes, assessment *practices* should not discriminate between students, and should set out not to disadvantage any individual or group. Obviously, students may prefer and do better at different kinds of assessment (some love exams and do well in them, while others are better at giving presentations, for example), so a balanced diet of different means of assessment within a course will set out to ensure that no particular group is favoured over any other group.

9   **Assessment should be formative – even when it is primarily intended to be summative.** Assessment is a time-consuming process for all con-cerned, so it seems like a wasted opportunity if it is not used as a means of letting students know how they are doing, and how they can improve. Assessment that is mainly summative in its function (for example, when only a number or grade is given) gives students very little information, other than frequently confirming their own prejudices about themselves.

10 **Formative assessment should start as early as possible in a course or module.** There is a great deal of research evidence that students benefit greatly by having some early feedback on how they are doing, and adjust their efforts accordingly. Conversely, if we leave assessment till too late, students who fail are frequently so discouraged that they drop out, or lose motivation.

11 **Assessment should be timely.** Assessment that occurs only at the end of a learning programme is not much use in providing feedback, and also leads to the 'sudden death' syndrome, meaning that students have no chance to practise before they pass or fail. Even where there is only end-point formal assessment, earlier opportunities should be provided for rehearsal and feedback.

12 **Assessment should be incremental.** Ideally, feedback to students should be continuous. There is sense therefore in enabling small units of assessment to build up into a final mark or grade. This avoids surprises, and can be much less stressful than systems in which the whole programme rests on performance during a single time-constrained occasion.

13 **Assessment should be redeemable.** Most universities insist that all assessment systems contain within them opportunities for the redemption of failure when things go wrong. This not only is just, but avoids high attrition rates.

14 **Assessment should be demanding.** Passing an assessment or test should not be automatic, and the assurance of quality is impossible when students are not stretched by assessment methods. That is not to say that systems should only permit a fixed proportion of students to achieve each grade; a good assessment system should permit all students considered capable of undertaking a course of study to have a chance of succeeding in the assessment, provided they learn effectively and work hard.

15 **Assessment should enable the demonstration of excellence.** The very best students should be able to be challenged to achieve at the highest standards.

16 **Assessment should be efficient and manageable.** It is possible to design brilliant systems of assessment that are nevertheless completely unmanageable because they make ineffective use of staff time and resources. The burden on staff should not be excessive, nor should be the demands on students undertaking the assessment tasks.

2

Why should we assess?

If we think clearly about our reasons for assessment, it helps to clarify which particular methods are best suited for our purposes, as well as helping to identify who is best placed to carry out the assessment, and when and where to do it. This section lists some of the most common reasons for assessing students. You might find it useful to look at these and decide which are the most important ones in the context of your own discipline, with your own students, at their particular level of study.

1 **To guide students' improvement.** The feedback students receive helps them to improve. Assessment that is primarily formative need not necessarily count towards any final award and can therefore be ungraded in some instances. The more detailed the feedback we provide, the greater is the likelihood that students will have opportunities for further development.

2 **To help students to decide which options to choose.** For example, if students have to select electives within a programme, an understanding of how well (or otherwise) they are doing in foundation studies will enable them to have a firmer understanding of their current abilities in different subject areas. This can provide them with guidance on which options to select next.

3 **To help students to learn from their mistakes or difficulties.** Many forms of formative assessment can be useful to students to help them to diagnose errors or weaknesses, and enable them to rectify mistakes. Nothing is more demotivating than struggling on getting bad marks and not knowing what is going wrong. Effective assessment lets students know where their problems lie, and provides them with information to help them to put things right.

4 **To allow students to check out how well they are developing as learners.** Assessment does not just test subject-specific skills and knowledge,

but provides an ongoing measure of how well students are developing their learning skills and techniques. Students themselves can use assessment opportunities to check out how they are developing their study skills and can make adjustments as appropriate.

5 **To classify or grade students.** There are frequently good reasons for us to classify the level of achievements of students individually and comparatively within a cohort. Assessment methods to achieve this will normally be summative and involve working out numerical marks or letter grades for students' work of one kind or another. However, continuous assessment processes can address the classifying or grading of students, yet still provide opportunities for formative developmental feedback along the way.

6 **To set standards.** The best way to estimate the standard of an educational course or module is to look at the various ways in which students' achievement is measured. The standard of the course is illustrated by the nature of the assessment tasks, and of course by the quality of students' work associated with the various tasks.

7 **To allow students to make realistic decisions about whether they are up to the demands of a course or module.** Students sometimes choose a module because they are interested in part of the subject, but then find that substantial parts of the module are too difficult for them, or not interesting enough. When the assessment profile of the module is clearly spelled out in advance, students can see how much the part they are interested in actually counts in the overall picture, and can be alerted to other important things they may need to master to succeed in the module.

8 **To determine fitness for entry to a programme.** Students often cannot undertake a course of study unless they have a sound foundation of prior knowledge or skills. Assessment methods to enable student progression therefore need to give a clear idea of students' current levels of achievement, so they – and we – can know if they are ready to move on.

9 **To give us feedback on how our teaching is going.** If there are generally significant gaps in student knowledge, these often indicate faults in the teaching of the areas concerned. Excellent achievement by a high proportion of students is often due to high-quality facilitation of student learning.

10 **To cause students to get down to some serious learning.** As students find themselves under increasing pressure, they tend to become more and more strategic in their approaches to learning, putting their energies only into work that counts. Assessment methods can be designed to maximise student motivation, and prompt their efforts towards important achievements.

11 **To translate intended learning outcomes into reality.** Assessment tasks and the feedback students receive on their work can show them what the intended learning outcomes mean in practice. Often it is only when students undertake tasks in which their evidence of achievement of the learning outcomes is being measured that they fully appreciate the nature and level of the competences they need to attain.

12 **To add variety to students' learning experience.** Utilising a range of different assessment methods spurs students to develop different skills and processes. This can promote more effective – and enjoyable – teaching and learning, and can help us to ensure that all students can demonstrate their strengths in those assessment contexts they find most comfortable and appropriate for them.

13 **To help us to structure our teaching and constructively align learning outcomes to assessments.** While 'teaching to the exam' is regarded as poor practice, it is very useful to keep in mind an overview of the various ways in which students' knowledge and skills will be assessed, so we can help students to strike a sensible balance regarding the time and energy they devote to each specific element of their study.

14 **To allow students to place themselves in the overall class picture.** Assessment can give students a frame of reference whereby they can compare their achievements with those of their peers. Students get a great deal of feedback from each other – more than their teachers can give them. Assessment helps them to find out how they are placed in the cohort, and can encourage them to make adjustments to get into a better position.

15 **To provide statistics for the course, or for the institution.** Educational institutions need to provide funding bodies and quality assurance agencies with data about student achievement and progression, and assessment systems need to take account of the need for appropriate statistical information.

16 **To lead towards a licence to practise.** In some professions, a degree or other qualification is taken as a measure of fitness to practise. It then becomes particularly important to ensure that validity and authenticity are achieved in the design of the assessment processes and instruments.

17 **To lead to appropriate qualifications.** Unlike some overseas universities, UK universities still maintain the degree classification system. However, some universities are continuing to ponder the introduction of a no-classifications system coupled with the production of student portfolios. Meanwhile, it is vitally important that we do everything we can to ensure that the students who deserve first-class degrees gain such awards, and that all students are judged fairly on the evidence of their achievement which we assess.

3

What are we assessing?
A checklist

Very often, we find that we are assessing not what we really want to assess, but what happens to be easy to assess. 'If you can assess it, it probably isn't it' is one way of summarising the dilemma. It's important, therefore, to be very clear about what we are actually committed to assess. To set you thinking, you can ask yourself the following questions about each assessment task you use.

1   **Is it product or process that is to be assessed? Or is it both?** Are we concentrating in this particular assessment task on the actual outcome (maybe a report, essay or artefact) or are we looking at how the students achieved the outcome?

2   **Are we assessing students' knowledge, or do we just assess the information they can give us back?** Einstein is reputed to have said, 'Knowledge is experience – everything else is just information.' It is therefore important to do what we can to measure knowledge and not just regurgitated information.

3   **Is it specific subject knowledge that we test, or is it how well students can apply such knowledge?** Does the method of assessment prioritise the need for information recall and regurgitation, or is the knowledge involved needed as a background for synthesis, analysis and evaluation by students?

4   **Is it individual effort or team effort that is to be assessed?** Teamwork is valued by employers, tutors and the students themselves, and sometimes it is most appropriate to assess students in groups. On other occasions, the performance of individuals needs to be most clearly differentiated.

5   **Is it teaching or learning that is being assessed?** Are the assessment tasks student centred? Are the tasks designed to allow students to demonstrate to what extent their learning has succeeded?

6   **Is assessment primarily formative or summative?** Are marks or grades needed by students at this point, or is this assessment task primarily there to allow students to receive feedback? There is little point in writing detailed comments on final-year degree scripts if students will never be able to read them! In many situations, however, assessment tasks can be designed to accommodate both formative and summative elements.

7   **Is the assessment convergent or divergent?** Are all students aiming to achieve identical results ('right answers'), or are the assessment tasks designed to enable students to demonstrate individuality and diversity? Both approaches may well be appropriate within a given course at different stages.

8   **Is the methodology continuous, cumulative or end point?** If it is continuous, there may be opportunities for redemption of failure without the risk on any particular element of assessment being too high. If assessment methodology is end point, then students will need to be made aware of this and prepared for it. If the assessment method is cumulative, are students clear about how the different elements build up to form a synoptic assigment?

9   **Does the assessment encourage deep, surface or strategic learning?** Encouraging deep learning has implications for course design. When students are overassessed, most will learn at a surface or strategic level only.

10   **Is the assessment holistic or serialist?** Does the assignment give students an opportunity to integrate material from a variety of sources, or is it a discrete element relating to a specific aspect of learning? Which approach is the more appropriate for the context in which you are working?

11   **Is the assessment time or context specific, or is it ipsative?** Does it measure achievement at a fixed point in time, or the extent of individuals' development from their earlier starting points?

12   **Is the assessment norm referenced or criterion referenced?** Does it measure a student's achievement in relation to that of other students, or does it enable students' achievements to be measured against a set of criteria? In the first instance, there is a tendency to have fixed pass/fail rates, whereas with criterion referencing, everyone who achieves the criteria will have passed.

4

When should we assess?

We have all encountered those stressful periods in an academic year when students feel overburdened with assessment and when we feel overstretched with marking. The following suggestions provide some alternatives to this.

1   **Start assessing early.** There is growing recognition that an early piece of coursework – or a short test – helps to prevent students from dropping out of courses or modules. Students need opportunities to find out whether they are up to the demands of their programmes, and feedback at this early stage can often cause them to get down to some serious study if needed, rather than just drifting on hoping it will all work out in the end.

2   **Consider starting diagnostic assessment before anything else.** Clearly, it would not be advisable for this kind of diagnostic assessment to count towards final qualifications, but it can give students a good idea about how their existing knowledge and experience place them, and of those areas to which they may need to pay particular attention. It can also help us to fine-tune the content and pace of our teaching; there is no point spending a lot of time covering things that most of the students can already achieve. However, avoid allowing diagnostic tests to be discouraging, particularly for non-traditional entrants to higher education.

3   **Spread the assessment out throughout the semester or year.** Bunching all assessments towards the end makes it very difficult for any formative feedback to be given to students. Without this, for example, students giving poor conclusions to essays could end up being marked down for the same fault on five or six occasions.

4   **Assess a little rather than a lot.** Save yourself time. Choose carefully what you really want to measure, and design tasks that measure this primarily. Don't measure the same knowledge or skills again and again. You can often

get just as good a comparative picture of how a class is doing from short assignments as you can from long, comprehensive ones.

5   **Time some assessments to cause students to get their heads around important concepts.** Even if the assessment element is short and easy to mark, and even if it does not count towards final grades, we can deliberately use such assessments to make sure that students spend that little bit more time and energy making sense of the concepts that we know they will need to master to enable them to understand the subject as they go more deeply into it.

6   **Give students agreed hand-in dates.** Then adhere to deadlines firmly. For example, say that a given assignment can only be marked if handed in on time. Offer to provide feedback but no marks when work is handed in late. In practice, however, make exceptions for documented illness, genuine crises, and so on, in line with the condonements policy of your own educational institution.

7   **Sometimes design formative assignments on things that students have not yet covered.** This can be a very effective way of alerting students to what they in due course need to learn. It helps students become more receptive when the topics concerned are addressed later in the taught programme.

8   **Try to time your assignments to avoid the 'week 7 nightmare'.** Students often report the phenomenon of everyone giving them coursework at the same time, and this time often falls around midway through a semester in modularised systems. In some universities, assessment dates are pre-planned, and timed to avoid such clashes, and are published at the beginning of each module.

9   **Continue to seek feedback from students about the timing of assessments.** It is worth continuing to ask students about any real problems they experience in meeting assessment deadlines. We can sometimes find out about problems we would not otherwise have known about.

5

Designing learning outcomes and linking them to assessment

Strong and demonstrable links between intended learning outcomes and assessment processes and criteria are central to the design of fit-for-purpose assessment. The work of John Biggs (2003) on 'constructive alignment' has helped many people to make such links explicit.

Ensuring that assessment is constructively aligned

Constructive alignment can be regarded as making sure that intended learning outcomes link well to evidence of students' achievement of the outcomes, to which are applied appropriate assessment criteria to assess students' achievement of the outcomes, and allowing students to receive direct and useful feedback on the extent to which they have demonstrated their achievement of the outcomes. A further important dimension of constructive alignment is to make informed decisions about what teaching and learning processes are most important to allow students to move towards achieving the learning outcomes and demonstrating that achievement in appropriate contexts.

In short, constructive alignment is about ensuring that assessment, teaching, learning and feedback are all in harmony with each other, and that feedback links well to students' evidence demonstrating their achievement of the intended learning outcomes. A visual way of thinking about this harmony is shown in Figure 1, adapted by Race as a 'slice' of his discussion of the 'ripples on a pond' model of learning (see Race, 2001c for the background to this). This provides a way of thinking about the need to link assessment and feedback to students' evidence of their achievement of the intended learning outcomes.

In the tips that follow, the design and use of learning outcomes will be considered first, so that a firm foundation can be set for the planning of assessment and the delivery of feedback to students.

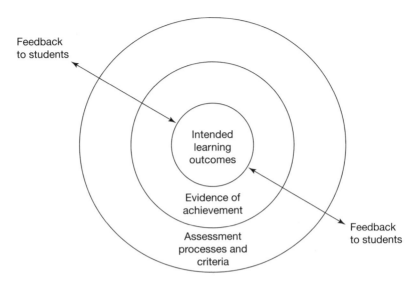

Figure 1 Linking learning outcomes, evidence of achievement, assessment criteria and feedback

Tips on designing and using learning outcomes

It is natural enough that professional people such as lecturers may feel some resistance to having the content of their teaching 'pinned down' by pre-expressed statements of intended learning outcome. However, the rationale for using such statements is so strong that we need to look at some practical pointers that will help even those who don't believe in them to be able to write them reasonably successfully. It is in the particularly public context of linking learning expressed outcomes to assessment criteria that most care needs to be taken.

1 **Help students to take ownership of the intended learning outcomes.** After all, it is they who are intended to achieve them, and it is their evidence of achievement of the outcomes that will be the basis of their exams and other assessed tasks. If students are very conscious of what they are intended to become able to do, they are much more likely to work systematically towards becoming able to give evidence of their achievement of the outcomes.

2 **Your intended learning outcomes should serve as a map to your teaching programme.** Students and others will look at the outcomes to see if the programme is going to be relevant to their needs or intentions. The level and standards associated with your course will be judged by reference to the stated learning outcomes.

3   **Don't set out to assess students' achievement of each and every learning outcome.** While there may indeed be an expectation (from professional bodies, quality assurance personnel, external reviewers, external examiners, and so on) that student achievement of the learning outcomes should be duly evidenced and tested, it is perfectly normal to test an appropriately representative cross-section of them rather than all of them in the context of a given cohort of students, and to aim to test all of them over a period of time across several student cohorts. That said, the most important learning outcomes need to be tested each time.

4   **Think ahead to assessment.** A well-designed set of learning outcomes should automatically become the framework for the design of assessed tasks. It is worth asking yourself, 'How can I measure this?' for each draft learning outcome. If it is easy to think of how it will be measured, you can normally go ahead and design the outcome. If it is much harder to think of how it could be measured, it is usually a signal that you may need to think further about the outcome, and try to relate it more firmly to tangible evidence that could be assessed.

5   **Aim to provide students with the whole picture.** Put the student-centred language descriptions of learning outcomes and assessment criteria into student handbooks, or turn them into a short self-contained leaflet to give to students at the beginning of the course. Ensure that students don't feel swamped by the shear size of the whole picture! Students need to be guided carefully through the picture in ways that allow them to feel confident that they will be able to succeed a step at a time.

6   **Don't get hung up too much on performance, standards and conditions** when expressing learning outcomes. For example, don't feel that such phrases as 'on your own' or 'without recourse to a calculator or computer' or 'under exam conditions' or 'with the aid of a list of standard integrals' need to be included in every well-expressed learning outcome. Such clarifications are extremely valuable elsewhere, in published assessment criteria.

7   **Don't confuse learning outcomes and assessment criteria.** It is best not to cloud the learning outcomes with the detail of performance criteria and standards until students know enough about the subject to understand the language of such criteria. In other words, the assessment criteria are best read by students *after* they have started to learn the topic, rather than at the outset (but make sure that the links will be clear in due course).

8   **Don't write any learning outcomes that can't (or won't) be assessed.** If it's important enough to propose as an intended learning outcome, it should be worthy of being measured in some way, and it should be *possible* to measure.

9   **Don't design any assessment task or question that is not related to the stated learning outcomes.** If it's important enough to measure, it is only fair to let students know that it is on their learning agenda.

10 **Don't state learning outcomes at the beginning and fail to return to them.** It's important to come back to them at the end of each teaching–learning element, such as lecture, self-study package, or element of practical work, and so on. Turn them into checklists for students – for example, along the lines 'Check now that you feel able to . . . ' or 'Now you should be in a position to . . . '

11 **Get students self-assessing their achievements.** Consider getting students to indicate, at the end of each learning element, the extent to which they feel that they have achieved the learning outcomes. For example, at the end of a lecture it can be useful to return to the slide or overhead on which the intended learning outcomes for that lecture were introduced, and, for each learning outcome in turn, ask students to 'vote' on how well they feel they have achieved them – for example, by raising both hands if they think they have fully achieved it, one hand if they feel they have partially achieved it, and no hands if they feel they have not yet achieved it. This gives you a good indication about which learning outcomes may need revisiting or consolidating in the next lecture, and so on.

6

Plagiarism, cheating and assessment

In a book about assessment, we must not forget that things can go wrong when students don't approach their tasks in the ways in which we intend them to do so. For assessment to work fairly, all parties must play the game. Plagiarism is usually interpreted as 'unfair or inappropriate usage of other people's work', while cheating is somewhat more sinister – though the borderlines between the two are impossible to define precisely. The following suggestions may help you to ensure that students know their responsibilities regarding fair play.

1   **Distinguish between malicious and inadvertent plagiarism.** Punitive action may be quite inappropriate when plagiarism is the consequence of students' lack of understanding of acceptable practice regarding citing the work of others.

2   **Debate issues and solutions with the whole class.** Establish ground rules for fair play, and agreed procedures for dealing with any infringements of these ground rules. It is important that such discussions should take place before the first assessment.

3   **Act decisively when you discover copying.** One option is to treat copying as collaborative work, and mark the work as normal but divide the total score by the number of students involved. Their reactions to this often help you find out who did the work first, or who played the biggest part in doing the work.

4   **Be alert when encouraging students to work together.** Make sure that they know where the intended collaboration should stop, and that you will be vigilant to check that later assessed work does not show signs of the collaboration having extended too far.

5   **Help students to understand the fine line between collaborative working and practices that the university will regard as cheating.**

Sometimes it can come as a shock and horror to students to find that what they thought of as acceptable collaboration is being regarded as cheating.

6   **Don't underestimate your students!** Clever students will always find a way to hack into computer-marked assessments. Bear this in mind when considering whether to use such processes for assessment or just for feedback. (If students can hack into the security systems of NASA, your system may not be as safe as you hope it is!).

7   **Anticipate problems and steer round them by briefing students on what is – and what isn't – plagiarism or cheating.** When collaboration is likely to occur, consider whether you can in fact turn it into a virtue by redesigning the assessments concerned to comprise collaborative tasks for students in groups.

8   **Be aware of cultural differences regarding acceptable behaviour regarding tests.** Bring the possibility of such differences to the surface by starting discussions with groups of students. Acknowledge and discuss the extreme pressures to avoid failure that some students may feel themselves subject to. Discuss with students the extent to which emulating their teachers and using their words is acceptable.

9   **Clarify your institution's requirements on fair practice.** Students actually *want* fair play, and can be very rigorous if asked to devise systems to guarantee this. Draw links between the systems and the assessment regulations extant in your university. Make sure that students understand what the regulations mean.

7

Monitoring the quality of assessment processes

However good we are at assessing students, we do well to monitor our effectiveness and keep a watching brief on what works well and what does not, so that we too can learn from our triumphs and mistakes, and can address problems. Quality reviewers, both internal and external, also look for evidence of how assessment quality is monitored.

1 **Interrogate your own assessment instruments and processes,** for example against the Quality Assurance Agency's 'Code of Practice'. (See www.qaa.ac.uk). This can lead to the discovery of important glitches, and the opportunity to improve assessment practice.

2 **Check that assessment is as inclusive as possible.** For example, in the United Kingdom the 'education exemption' of the 1995 Disabilities Discrimination Act was repealed with effect from 2002 by the Special Educational Needs and Disabilities Act (SENDA). The legislation now requires us to make 'reasonable adjustments' so that all students can have optimum opportunity to demonstrate their achievement of the learning outcomes via ways in which having special needs does not disadvantage them. Furthermore, we are now legally required to make any necessary adjustments in an *anticipatory* manner, rather than wait to see if anyone seems to be being disadvantaged.

3 **Keep an overview of the marks you are giving.** In a small sample, it won't be possible to get a set of results that plot into a normal distribution curve on a graph. However, if you notice that all your marks are bunching too tightly at the median point, or that everyone is getting top marks, this may indicate that something is awry. It may help you to use a spreadsheet or other visual means to keep an eye on what's going on.

4 **Get students to give you feedback on how well they feel you are assessing them.** You may not always want to hear their answers, but you

could ask questions, including 'Am I giving you enough feedback?', 'Do you find it helps you to improve?', 'Is the turnaround fast enough for you?', 'Is there any way in which I can improve my assessment?', 'How useful are the questions I am setting?', and so on.

5   **Get help from colleagues.** In the rare cases when work is not double-marked, sampled or moderated, it is useful to get colleagues to take a look at some of your grades, particularly when you are inexperienced regarding assessment. Pick scripts including a strong one, a weak one and an average one, and ask an experienced colleague or two to confirm that they agree with your evaluation.

6   **Keep notes from year to year.** As you assess sets of work, note any difficulties you experience that may have arisen from the timing of the assessment or how you briefed the students. Note also difficulties of interpretation. Use these notes to help you design better assessments in future years.

7   **Remember how valuable data on student performance are in their own right.** Use such data to identify areas where students generally showed strengths and weaknesses. Such data represent important evidence for external or internal quality review. Think ahead regarding how future assessments may be adjusted to help students to address areas of weakness next time round.

8   **Beware of upward-creeping standards.** The more experienced you become in teaching and assessing a subject, the greater the risk that you gradually expect or demand higher levels of performance from successive groups of students.

9   **Tune in to other universities.** Build up your list of friends and colleagues in other colleges and exchange with them past exam papers, assignment briefings and marking schemes. This can help you to design new tasks more easily for your own students, and also gives you the chance to seek feedback from such people on your own assessment practices.

10 **Stand back and ask, 'What did that really measure?'** When reflecting on data from assignment performances or exam results, check that you did in fact succeed in measuring those aspects of student performance that you intended to assess. Also, however, ask, 'What *else* did I measure?' Decide whether next time to make such additional agendas more explicit when they are valuable (or, when they are not valuable, how to steer assessment tasks away from such agendas).

11 **Make constructive use of comments from external assessors.** Quality auditors or reviewers, external examiners and others may well provide you

with comments on how effectively they perceive your assessment methods to be. Use such feedback to help you to improve continuously, rather than seeing it as a personal attack. Make sure that you continue to include those elements that they praise or commend, and develop such elements further when appropriate.

12 **Consider trying to become an external assessor yourself.** Once you have developed expertise in your own university, an excellent way to learn from the experiences of other institutions is to become involved in external examining or quality-reviewing yourself. What you learn about the excellence (or otherwise) of others' means of assessment can then be transferred to your own context.

8

Don't assess like this!

The suggestions that follow are tongue in cheek. They are designed to get you thinking about what can actually get in the way of students' learning. You may wish to show them to your students and ask them why the advice given here is seriously misguided. Such a discussion may play its part in helping students to understand what is really expected of them in assessment. Furthermore, you may find it interesting to interrogate these suggestions against the values we offered at the start of this chapter, and analyse how each of these suggestions actually violates these values.

1 **Keep your students in the dark about the rules of the game.** Brighter students will intuitively understand the criteria and naturally excel. You will thereby get a good range of marks, from the truly appalling to the really outstanding. This will make your external examiner happy.

2 **Carry out all assessment at the end of the learning programme.** You can't assess students until you have taught them everything, so all the assessment needs to take place at the very end of the process. If they then fail, it just shows that they aren't very good.

3 **Make sure that you know the identity of the student who has done each element of work.** Then you can check whether the standard is what you would expect of that student. You can then adjust marks if you think that a poor student has overperformed, or a strong student has not done himself or herself justice. You can normally tell pretty well early on what kind of a degree a student will get, and such expectations are rarely proved wrong.

4 **To be fair to all students, give each an identical test.** If they have problems with it because of so-called special needs, that's their problem.

5   **For coursework assessments, stick firmly to your deadlines.** Don't take any notice of the plausible excuses students will come up with. The real world works on deadlines. If you show any flexibility, students will just take advantage of you.

6   **Don't be soft on any students who claim that they don't do well in exams.** Even if their coursework marks are good, remind them that they have to get their act together for exams, or else they shouldn't be in higher education in the first place.

7   **Don't give students any written feedback.** They will only argue with you about the marks you have given them and ask you to justify how your comments link to the scores you have awarded. You can't be expected to do that; in fact, it is probably safest just to give them the mark and never give them back their original work.

8   **Always plan at least some questions on material that you haven't covered with the class.** This sorts out those students who read around the subject from those who don't. But don't actually tell them that this is what you're planning to do, or the strategic students may read around.

9   **When you set coursework essays, don't set a word limit.** The good students will naturally have a lot to say, and will deserve high marks. You can usually tell at once from the length of an essay how much thought has gone into it.

10 **Don't make your questions too straightforward.** You want to be able to see who can make sense of the questions, so you can give these students the higher marks. Students who can't make sense of a question are demonstrating their ignorance, and don't deserve high marks.

11 **Don't get into discussions with a class about how they will be assessed.** Just remind them that they're there to learn and you're here to teach them, and that they've got to give you proof of what they've learned.

12 **If you design a question paper that works well, use it year on year.** You can save yourself a lot of work by using the same questions again and again. There is no need to worry about students from previous years talking to the next cohort of students as they all tend to lead quite separate lives.

Reminder: the above is what *not* to do! We've put these suggestions in a box to make this distinction clearer. These suggestions are adapted from an article by Sally Brown, in 2004 for the University of Gloucestershire.

9

'I wish I hadn't done that!'

This section includes some illustrative examples learned from ourselves and from colleagues who have made various mistakes in designing assessment instruments or practices. We include these scenarios in the hope that they may help others avoid making similar mistakes, and that they will whet your appetite for some of the more detailed suggestions and discussions we offer in the chapters that follow.

1   **The assignment that required high level mathematics.** In an attempt to ensure fairness in undertaking self- and peer assessment components of a group assignment, some marks were allocated for individual contributions, others for group contributions. Using a combination of self-assessment, intra-peer assessment (students assessing members of their own group), inter-peer assessment (students assessing other groups) and tutor assessment, the tutor ended up awarding total marks out of 280, and had to do a great deal of adding up and averaging. Later versions of the assessment ensured that it was much simpler!

2   **The tutor who got caught in the crossfire.** A colleague stuck strictly to the handbook requirements when assessing student work, and a group of students complained that the rules were too harsh and didn't take into account individual difficulties. When the tutor responded that she had no flexibility within the university system, the students took out a formal complaint against her. She wished she had not let herself get caught up in defending the assessment regulations, and had instead referred the original student complaints upwards through the institution.

3   **The tutor who allowed heart to get in the way of head.** A student with language difficulties complained to his lecturer that all the other lecturers 'had it in for him' and were marking him down. Without investigating further, she was vociferous in his defence at the course team meeting, only to find that the student concerned had been given lots of well-documented support

by several course team members over the year, and that what he had told her was simply untrue.

4   **The tutor who agreed to 'just look through my first draft please'.** Having given one student a lot of detailed formative feedback on an individual basis, she found a group of other students who wanted similar levels of support. She felt she could not in fairness fail to support them in the way that she had the first student, and consequently was overwhelmed by the demands made upon her time.

5   **The tutor who took all his marking home.** A colleague assiduously marked a pile of student essays, completed the paperwork and put everything in the boot of his car to take back to college next day. His car was stolen overnight and torched. He wished that he had either kept the mark sheet in the house, or emailed it to himself at work. Similar tales include that of the tutor whose goat ate the assignments, the tutor whose husband took the bag of marked scripts to the recycling bin, the tutor whose briefcase was stolen on the train, the tutor who hand-delivered, for safety, the marked scripts to the empty house next door to where the external examiner lived – and so on!

6   **The tutor who went his own way.** Confident that he had been marking students' work at this level for many years, a tutor decided he didn't need to go to the briefing meeting for a jointly marked assignment. When he had completed all his assessments, he found that his marks were out of kilter with those of his colleagues, because he had failed to understand that the agreed weighting of criteria was different from that in previous years. He then had to do a lot of work adjusting his marks to meet the agreed procedures.

7   **The tutor who didn't give students a limit as to how much they should include in their portfolios.** As a consequence, he received a vast amount of extraneous material from each student, and had to wade through all of this before he could assign marks, and could only physically carry half a dozen of the 87 portfolios home at any one time.

8   **The tutor who asked students to write a reflective account based on their own personal experiences of a tragic event.** The marking proved so distressing for the tutor that it took an inordinate amount of time and left her feeling drained and depressed. Also, she could not disassociate her sympathy for some of the tragedies her students had suffered from her marking, and found herself wanting to compensate the students who had suffered most by giving them additional marks.

9   **The tutor who left all the marking till the last possible minute.** Several versions of this sad tale exist, including the tutor going down with flu, or the tutor whose spouse arranged a special surprise anniversary weekend away, or the numerous tales where a family crisis occurred just at the wrong time (don't they always?).

Chapter 2

Exams of various sorts

10 Traditional unseen, time-constrained written exams
11 Open-book exams
12 Open-notes exams
13 Structured exams
14 Vivas – oral exams
15 Some other kinds of examination

10

Traditional unseen, time-constrained written exams

'Unseen' means that candidates don't know what the exam questions will be until they are sitting at their desks in the exam room. 'Time-constrained' means 'against the clock', and the possibility of at least some of the students not being able to complete their answers to all questions in the time allowed.

Such exams still make up the lion's share of assessment in higher education, though in many disciplines this situation is considerably balanced by the inclusion of practical work, projects and other contributions to the evidence on the basis of which we grade and classify students. Notwithstanding growing concern about the validity and fairness of traditional exams, for all sorts of reasons they will continue to play a large part in the overall assessment picture. Despite the concerns about exams, we aim in the following discussion to suggest a number of ways that the use of exams can be improved, recognising that they continue to be valuable in a variety of contexts.

Table 1 Advantages and disadvantages of assessment via traditional time-constrained unseen written exams

Advantages	Disadvantages
• **Relatively economical.** Exams can be more cost-effective than many of the alternatives (though this depends on economies of scale when large numbers of students are examined, and also on how much time and money need to be spent to ensure appropriate moderation of assessors' performance). • **Equality of opportunity.** Exams are demonstrably fair in that students all	• **Can have low validity.** If what students can write about what they remember about what they read is all that is being measured, validity is poor. • **Students get little or no feedback** about the detail of their performance, which is therefore a wasted opportunity as far as feedback is concerned. Though it can be argued that the purpose of exams is measurement rather than feedback, the

Table 1 continued

Advantages	Disadvantages
have the same tasks to do in the same way and within the same timescale.	counter-argument is that most exams, to some extent, represent lost learning opportunities because of this lack of
• **We know whose work it is.** It is easier to be sure that the work being assessed was done by the candidate, and not by other people. For this reason, exams are considered by some to be an 'anti-plagiarism assessment' device.	feedback. Where students are given the opportunity to see their marked scripts (even with no more feedback than seeing the sub-totals and total marks awarded along the way), they learn a great deal about exactly what went wrong with some of their answers, as well as having
• **Teaching staff are familiar with exams.** Familiarity does not always equate with validity, but the base of experience that teaching staff already have with traditional unseen exams means that at least some of the problems arising from them are well known, and sometimes well addressed.	the chance to receive confirmation regarding the questions they answered well. • **Badly set exams encourage surface learning,** with students consciously clearing their minds of one subject as they prepare for exams in the next subject. In many discipline areas, it is inappropriate to encourage students to put out of their minds important subject
• **Exams cause students to get down to learning.** Even if the assessment method has problems, it certainly causes students to engage deliberately with the subject matter being covered by exams, and this can be worthwhile, particularly for those 'harder' discipline areas where students might not otherwise spend the time and energy that are needed to make sense of the subject matter.	matter, because they will need to retain their mastery for later stages in their studies. • **Technique is too important.** Exams tend to measure how good students are at answering exam questions, rather than how well they have learned. The consequence is that those students who become skilled at exam technique are rewarded time after time, while other students who may have mastered the subject material to a greater degree may not get due credit for their learning if their exam technique repeatedly lets them down.
	• **Exams only represent a snapshot of student performance,** rather than a reliable indicator of it. How students perform in traditional exams depends on many factors apart from their grasp of the subject being tested. Students' state of mind on the day, their luck or otherwise in tackling a good question first, their state of health, and many other irrelevant factors creep in.

Setting unseen written exam questions

Many experienced assessors remember with some horror the first time they put pen to paper to write exam questions. Sometimes they felt well equipped to do so, as they had been involved in exams as candidates for most of their lives, and thought that it was quite straightforward to write good questions. But then the realisation dawned that the words and tasks used in exam questions could determine students' future careers, prospects, incomes and lifestyles. Often, only on the first occasion when they mark exam scripts do lecturers first become aware of just how sensitively the questions need to be designed, and how clearly the assessment criteria and marking schemes need to be laid out to anticipate as many as possible of the different ways that even the most unambiguous-looking question can turn out to be answered in practice. The suggestions that follow can help to spare you from some of the headaches that can result from hastily written exam questions.

1 **Don't do it on your own!** Make sure you get feedback on each of your questions from colleagues. They can spot whether your question is at the right level more easily than you can. Having someone else look at one's draft exam questions is extremely useful, and it is better still when all questions are discussed and moderated by teams of staff. Where possible, draft questions *with* your colleagues. This allows the team to pick the best questions from a range of possibilities, rather than use every idea each member has.

2 **Ask colleagues, 'What would you say this question really means?'** If they tell you anything you hadn't thought of, you may need to adjust your wording a little.

3 **Get one or two colleagues to *do* your questions – or do them yourself!** Sometimes even sketch answers can be helpful. This may be asking a lot of busy colleagues, but the rewards can be significant. You will often find that they answered a particular question in a rather different way from the one you had in mind when you designed the question. Being alerted in advance to the ways that different students might approach a question gives you the opportunity to accommodate alternative approaches in your marking scheme, or to adjust the wording of your question so that your intended or preferred approach is made clear to students.

4 **Have your intended learning outcomes in front of you as you draft your questions.** It is all too easy to dream up interesting questions that turn out to be tangential to the learning outcomes. Furthermore, it is possible to write too many questions addressing particular learning outcomes, leaving other outcomes unrepresented in the exam.

5 **Keep your sentences short.** You're less likely to write something that can be interpreted in more than one way if you write plain English in short

sentences. This also helps reduce any discrimination against those students for whom English is their second or third language.

6 **Work out what you're really testing.** Is each question measuring decision-making, strategic planning, problem-solving, data processing (and so on), or is it just too dependent on memory? Most exam questions measure a number of things at the same time. Be up-front about all the things each question is likely to measure. In any case, external scrutiny of assessment may interrogate whether your questions (and your assessment criteria) link appropriately with the published learning outcomes for your course or module.

7 **Don't measure the same things again and again.** For example, it is all too easy in essay-type exam questions to repeatedly measure students' skills at writing good introductions, firm conclusions and well-structured arguments. Valuable as such skills are, we need to be measuring other important things too.

8 **Include data or information in questions to reduce the emphasis on memory.** In some subjects, case-study information is a good way of doing this. Science exams often tend to be much better than other subjects in this respect, and it is appropriate to be testing what candidates can *do* with data rather than how well they remember facts and figures.

9 **Make the question layout easy to follow.** A question with bullet points or separate parts can be much easier for (tense) candidates to interpret correctly than one that is just several lines of continuous prose.

10 **Don't overdo the standards.** When you're close to a subject, it's easily possible that your questions get gradually harder year by year. For example, in exams including quantitative questions, there is the danger that numerical problems become more difficult in each successive exam, partly because of the wish to stretch students a little further than did the worked examples they may have seen in lectures, or the problems students tackled in tutorials.

11 **Check the timing.** You'll sometimes find that it takes *you* an hour to answer a question for which candidates have only half an hour. Assessors setting problem-type questions for students often forget that familiarity with the type of problem profoundly influences the time it takes to solve it. Students who get stuck on such a question may end up failing the exam more through time mismanagement than through lack of subject-related competence.

12 **Decide what the assessment criteria will be.** Check that these criteria relate clearly to the syllabus objectives or the intended learning outcomes. Make it your business to ensure that students themselves are clear about these

objectives or intended outcomes, and emphasise the links between these and assessment. When students are aware that the expressed learning outcomes are a template for the design of assessment tasks, it is possible for them to make their learning much more focused.

13   **Work out a tight marking scheme for yourself.** Imagine that you are going to delegate the marking to a new colleague. Write the marking scheme down. You will find such schemes an invaluable aid to share with future classes of students, as well as colleagues actually co-marking with you; they help them to see how assessment works.

14   **Use the question itself to show how marks are to be allocated.** For example, put numbers in brackets to show how many marks are attached to various parts of the question (or alternatively, give suggested timings such as 'spend about ten minutes on Part 2').

15   **Proof-read your exam questions carefully.** Be aware of the danger of seeing what you *meant*, rather than what you actually *wrote*! Even if you're very busy when asked to check your questions, a little extra time spent editing your questions at this time may save you many hours sorting out how to handle matters arising from any ambiguities or errors that could have otherwise slipped through the proof-reading process.

Designing marking schemes

Constructing a good marking scheme can save you hours when it comes to marking a pile of scripts. It can also help you to know (and show) that you are doing everything possible to be uniformly fair to all students. As your marking schemes will normally be shown to external examiners and quality reviewers, among other people, it's important to design schemes in the first place so that they will stand up to such scrutiny. The following suggestions should help.

1   **Write a model answer for each question, if the subject matter permits.** This can be a useful first step towards identifying the mark-bearing ingredients of a good answer. It also helps you see when what you thought was going to be a 30-minute question turns out to take an hour. If you have difficulties answering the questions, the chances are that your students will too! Making model answers and marking schemes for coursework assignments can give you good practice for writing exam schemes.

2   **Make each decision as straightforward as possible.** Try to allocate each mark so that it is associated with something that is either present or absent, or right or wrong, in students' answers.

3 **Aim to make your marking scheme usable by a non-expert in the subject.** This can help your marking schemes be useful resources for students themselves, perhaps in next year's course.

4 **Aim to make it so that anyone can mark given answers and agree on the scores within a mark or two.** It is best to involve colleagues in your piloting of first-draft marking schemes. They will soon help you to identify areas where the marking criteria may need clarifying or tightening up.

5 **Allow for 'consequential' marks.** For example, when a candidate makes an early mistake but then proceeds correctly thereafter (especially in problems and calculations), allow for some marks to be given for the ensuing correct steps even when the final answer is quite wrong.

6 **Pilot your marking scheme by showing it to others.** It's worth even showing marking schemes to people who are not closely associated with your subject area. If they can't see exactly what you're looking for, it may be that the scheme is not yet sufficiently self-explanatory. Extra detail you add at this stage may help you to clarify your own thinking, and will certainly assist fellow markers.

7 **Consider having more than 20 marks for a 20-mark question.** Especially in essay-type answers, you can't expect students to include all the things you may think of yourself. It may be worth having up to 30 or more 'available' marks, so that students approaching the question in different ways still have the opportunity to score well.

8 **Look at what others have done in the past.** If it's your first time writing a marking scheme, looking at other people's ways of doing them will help you to focus your efforts. Choose to look at marking schemes from other subjects that your students may be studying, to help you tune in to the assessment culture of the overall course.

9 **Learn from your own mistakes.** No marking scheme is perfect. When you start applying it to a pile of scripts, you will soon start adjusting it. Keep a note of any difficulties you experience in adhering to your scheme, and take account of these next time you have to make one.

Marking examination scripts

The following suggestions may help you approach the task of marking exam scripts efficiently, while still being fair and helpful to students.

1 **Be realistic about what you can do.** Marking scripts can be boring, exhausting and stressful. As far as constraints allow, don't attempt to mark

large numbers of scripts in short periods of time. Put scripts for marking into manageable bundles. It is less intimidating to have ten scripts on your desk and the rest out of sight than to have the whole pile threatening you as you work.

2   **Devise your own system of tackling the marking load.** You may prefer to mark a whole script at a time, or just question 1 of every script first. Do what you feel comfortable with, and see what works best for you.

3   **Avoid halo effects.** If you've just marked a brilliant answer on a script, it can be easy to go into the *same* student's next answer seeing only the good points and passing over the weaknesses. Try to ensure that you mark each answer dispassionately. Conversely, when you look at the *next* student's answer, you may be over-critical if you've just marked a brilliant one.

4   **Watch out for prejudices.** There will be all sorts of things that you like and dislike about the style and layout of scripts, not to mention handwriting quality. Make sure that each time there is a 'benefit of the doubt' decision to be made, it is not influenced by such factors.

5   **Recognise that your mood will change.** Every now and then, check back to scripts you marked earlier, and see whether your generosity has increased or decreased. Be aware of the middle-mark bunching syndrome. As you get tired, it feels safe and easy to give a middle-range mark. Try as far as possible to look at each script afresh.

6   **Remind yourself of the importance of what you're doing.** You may be marking a whole pile of scripts, but each individual script may be a crucial landmark in the life of the student concerned. Your verdict may affect students for the rest of their careers.

7   **Take account of the needs of second markers.** Many universities and colleges use a blind double-marking system, in which case you should not make any written comments or numbers on the scripts themselves to avoid prejudicing the judgement of a second marker (unless of course photocopies have already been made of each script for double marking). You may find it useful to use Post-it™ notes or assessment pro formas for each script so that at any later stage you are able to justify the marks you give. Such *aides-mémoires* can save you having to read the whole scripts again, rethinking how you arrived at your numbers or grades.

8   **Write a feedback report for students.** In most exams the system may not allow you to write on the scripts the sort of feedback you would have given if the questions had been set as assessed coursework. However, students still need feedback, and making notes for yourself of the things you would have

explained about common mistakes can help you prepare some discussion notes to issue to students after the exam, or can remind you of things to mention next time you teach the same subjects.

9   **Provide feedback for yourself and for the course team.** As you work through the scripts, note how many students answered each question, and how well they performed. You may begin to realise that some questions have turned out to be very well written, while others could have been framed better. You will find out which questions proved to be the hardest for students to answer well, even when all questions were intended to be of an equal standard. Such feedback and reflection should prove very useful when designing questions next time round.

10 **Set aside time for a review.** Having marked all the scripts, you may wish to capture your thoughts, such as suggestions about changes for part of the course or module, or the processes used to teach it. It is really useful, however tired you feel, to write a short draft report on the marking as soon as you have completed it. Otherwise, important things that are still fresh in your tired mind will all too quickly evaporate.

Helping students to see what their exams may measure

The checklist in Table 2 is adapted from an exercise to set students when running study-skills sessions for them on revision strategies and exam technique. The original exercise, with discussion, is in Race (1999).

Table 2 Task: what do you think traditional exams really measure? Make your decisions below, then compare your views to those of other people – particularly those who mark exams.

Factors measured by time-constrained unseen written exams?	Measured very well	Measured to some extent	Not really measured
1 How much you know about your subject?			
2 How much you *don't* know about your subject?			
3 The *quantity* of revision that you will have done?			
4 The *quality* of revision that you will have done?			

Table 2 continued

Factors measured by time-constrained unseen written exams?	Measured very well	Measured to some extent	Not really measured
5 How intelligent you are?			
6 How much work you did the night before?			
7 How well you keep your cool?			
8 How good your memory is?			
9 How good you are at question-spotting?			
10 How fast you think?			
11 How fast you write?			
12 How legible your handwriting is?			
13 How good you are at answering exam questions?			
14 How carefully you read the questions?			
15 How wisely you choose the questions that you attempt?			
16 How well you manage your time *during* exams?			
17 How well you keep exactly to the questions in your answers?			
18 How well you set out your answers to the questions?			
19 How skilled you are at solving problems?			
20 How carefully you read your answers after writing them?			
21 How well you edit/improve your answers after reading them?			

Using exam questions as class exercises

Answering exam questions well is still one of the principal skills that students need to develop to succeed in their studies in most subjects. The checklist (Table 2) is one way of alerting students to the big picture of exams, but it is well worth going further and letting them find out more detail about what exams actually measure in the context of their particular discipline or topic. In our attempts to increase the learning pay-off of taught sessions, we can help students to develop their exam skills by making use of past exam questions. The following suggestions may help you to build related activities into your lectures and tutorials – but don't try to implement more than two or three of these suggestions with any one cohort; you haven't got time!

1   **Let a class have a try at an exam question under exam conditions.** Then ask students to exchange their answers, and lead them through marking their work using a typical marking scheme. This helps students to learn quickly how examiners' minds work. It is well worth using the whole of at least one lecture slot for such an exercise; the learning pay-off for students is likely to be considerably more than if you'd just spent an extra hour with one small element of their curriculum.

2   **Issue two or three previous exam questions for students to try in preparation for a tutorial.** Then lead them through an assessment of their work using a marking scheme during the tutorial. Ask them to prepare lists of questions on matters arising from the exercise, on both subject content and requirements for exams, and use their questions to focus tutorial discussion.

3   **Display an exam question on-screen in a large-group lecture.** Ask students in groups to brainstorm the principal steps they would take in the way they would approach answering the question. Then give out a model answer to the question as a handout and talk the class through the points in the model answer where marks would be earned. All this can be achieved in less than half of the overall time of a typical lecture, and you may be surprised at the levels of interest and attention that students pay to such elements in a lecture slot.

4   **In a lecture or a tutorial, get students in groups to think up exam questions themselves.** You can base this on work they have already covered, or on work currently in progress. Ask the groups to transcribe their questions onto overhead transparencies. Display each of these in turn, giving feedback on how appropriate or otherwise each question is in terms of standard, wording, length and structure. (You will get many questions this way that you can later use or adapt for next year's exams or future course-work assignments.)

5   **Use exam questions to help students to create an agenda.** In a lecture or tutorial, give out two or three related exam questions as a handout. Ask students in groups to make lists of short questions that they don't yet know the answers to. Then allow the groups to use you as a resource, quizzing you with these questions. You don't have to answer them all at once – for some, your reply will be along the lines 'We'll come to this in a week or two', and for others 'You won't actually be required to know this.'

6   **Get students to make marking schemes.** Give them a typical exam question and ask groups of students to prepare a breakdown of how they think the marks should be allocated. Ask them to transcribe the marking schemes to overhead transparencies. Discuss each of these in turn with the whole group, and give guidance as to how closely the marking schemes resemble those used in practice.

7   **Get students to surf the Net.** Ask them to look for appropriate exam questions on the subjects they are studying. Suggest that they work in twos or threes and bring the questions they find to the next class session. Encourage them to download the questions and make an electronic question bank.

8   **Ask students in groups to think up 'dream' and 'nightmare' questions.** Ask the groups to make bullet-point lists of the ten most important things that they would include in answers to the 'dream' questions. These questions will give you useful information about their favourite topics. Use 'nightmare' questions to open up discussion of the causes of their anxieties, and point them in the right direction regarding how they might tackle such questions.

9   **Ask students to think of way-out, alternative questions.** Suggest that they think of questions that do not merely test their knowledge and skills, but get them to think laterally and creatively. This encourages deeper reflection about the material they are learning, and will probably give you some interesting ideas to use in future exams.

Helping students to cope with exam failure

Of course we'd all prefer that such help was not needed. However, in most exam systems, casualties seem inevitable. The fact that some students did not pass does not mean that they could not have passed. The following suggestions may help you to guide students who failed towards future successes.

1   **Help students to come to a position where they can see failure as an opportunity for learning.** This is better than the natural instinct that leads

37

people to regard failure as a major disaster. Failing an exam can be a strong demotivator, but can also be an opportunity to seek feedback, providing a stimulus for deeper learning.

2   **Take account of the feelings of students.** Students who fail exams often take it as a blow to their self-esteem. Be prepared for a whole range of resultant emotions, including anger, inertia, disbelief and inconsolable grief. For students who have done well at school, failing exams at university may be their first experiences of failure, and can give them a profound shock. For those who struggled to get to university, exam failure may confirm their underlying suspicion that they were never quite up to it in the first place.

3   **Help students to understand that it is their *work* and not their personality that is the problem.** Try to focus any feedback on their practices rather than their personal qualities, to avoid damage to their self-esteem.

4   **Concentrate on what students can do in future to improve, rather than railing over their failings.** Let students see a range of examples of satisfactory and good work (rather than just model answers, which imply the need for perfection). Help students to see how their answers could be made more like the examples you provide.

5   **Let students have further opportunities for practising under simulated exam conditions.** Ideally, this can give students the chance to experience success before they next experience real exams.

6   **Let students play examiner.** Give students the chance to apply assessment schemes to examples of good, bad and indifferent exam scripts (and, if possible, to their own scripts that failed). This process rapidly increases students' awareness of the rules of the exam game.

7   **Help students to identify what went well.** Even in a failed exam, most students display strengths in some parts of some questions. Help them not to dismiss these strengths in the context of their overall failure, and encourage them to extend the areas of success on future occasions.

8   **Help students develop revision and exam techniques.** There are plenty of books, learning packages and computer packages available to help students to build up confidence.

9   **Encourage students in pairs to set each other questions and mark them.** Informally talking through their answers to each other can motivate them, and help them improve their self-confidence.

10 **Give students the chance to recognise that your course or module might be wrong for them.** If they decide to move on to another subject or field of study, then help them to recognise that their move may be down to having originally made a poor choice of subject to study, rather than its necessarily being the result of any lack of ability or intelligence on their part.

11

Open-book exams

In many ways, open-book exams are similar to traditional exams, but with the major difference that students are allowed to take in with them sources of reference material. Alternatively, candidates may be issued with a standard set of resource materials that they can consult during the exam, and are informed in advance about what will be available to them, so that they can prepare themselves by practising to apply the resource materials. Sometimes in addition, the 'timed' element is relaxed or abandoned, allowing students to answer questions with the aid of their chosen materials and at their own pace.

Table 3 Advantages and disadvantages of assessment via open-book exams

Advantages	Disadvantages
Open-book exams have many of the advantages of traditional exams, with the addition of: • **Less stress on memories!** The emphasis is taken away from students being required to remember facts, figures, formulae, and other such information. • **Can be higher on validity.** Effective questions can measure what students can *do* with the content of the books, rather than their simply recalling it or rewriting it. • **Measuring retrieval skills.** It is possible to set questions that measure how well students can use and apply information, and how well they can find their way round the contents of books and even databases.	• **Not enough books or resources!** It is hard to ensure that all students are equally equipped regarding the books they bring into the exam with them. Limited stocks of library books (and the impossibility of students purchasing their own copies of expensive books) mean that some students may be disadvantaged. • **Need bigger desks?** Students necessarily require more desk space for open-book exams if they are to be able to use several sources of reference as they compose their answers to exam questions. This means fewer students can be accommodated in a given exam room than with traditional unseen exams, and therefore open-book exams are rather less cost-effective in terms of accommodation and invigilation.

Table 3 continued

Advantages	Disadvantages
• **Slower writers helped?** If coupled with a relaxation in the timed dimension (e.g. a nominal 'two-hour' paper but with students being allowed to spend up to three hours if they wish), some of the pressure is taken away from those students who happen to be slower at writing down their answers (and also students who happen to think more slowly). Dyslexic students and those with disabilities might particularly welcome this flexibility.	• **Too much time may be spent on finding out which parts of the books to use.** However, if students are given the chance to *practise* using the books, this disadvantage can be reduced. • **Badly briefed students may use the wrong approach.** They may continue to approach the exam as though it were memory based.

Setting open-book exam questions

Most of the suggestions given earlier about setting traditional exam questions continue to apply to designing open-book questions. In addition:

1 **Decide whether to prescribe the books students may employ.** This is one way round the problem of availability of books. It may even be possible to arrange supplies of the required books to be available in the exam room.

2 **Consider compiling a source collection for the particular exam.** Check on copyright issues and see whether it is cost-effective to put together a set of papers, extracts, data and other information from which students can find what they need to address the questions in the particular exam.

3 **Set questions that require students to do things with the information available to them,** rather than merely to locate the correct information and then summarise it or give it back.

4 **Make the actual questions particularly clear and straightforward to understand.** The fact that students will be reading a lot during the exam means that care has to be taken that they don't read the actual instructions too rapidly.

5 **Plan for shorter answers.** Students doing open-book exams will be spending quite a lot of their time searching for, and making sense of, information and data. They will therefore write less per hour than students who are answering traditional exam questions 'out of their heads'.

12

Open-notes exams

Open-notes exams are similar to open-book exams, described in the previous section,, except that students are allowed to bring into the examination room not books, but any notes that *they* have prepared for the purpose. In other words, we are talking about a situation of 'legitimised crib-notes'! Your first thought may be that this is all very strange, but in fact such exams can work surprisingly well. Many of the advantages of and suggestions for open-book exams continue to apply, but the additional advantages and disadvantages arise as summarised in Table 4.

Table 4 Advantages and disadvantages of assessment via open-notes exams

Advantages	Disadvantages
• **Students can achieve a very significant learning pay-off simply making the notes in the first place.** The act of making revision summaries can have high learning pay-off. It is best not to place stringent limits on the amount of materials that students can bring in. Those who bring in everything they have ever written about your topic will be disadvantaging themselves in that it will take them much longer to search for the relevant parts of their notes, compared to students who have been really selective in summarising the important parts of your topic. Advise students of this in advance. • **The emphasis on memory is reduced, allowing competence to be tested more effectively.** Open-notes exams can also spread candidates' abilities out more fairly, as the better candidates will have made better notes in the first place.	• **Students need rehearsal at preparing for open-notes exams.** They may take two or three practice runs to develop the art of making comprehensive but manageable summaries of the important data or information you intend them to make available to themselves. • **Candidates whose open notes were not very suitable are penalised quite severely.** Some of these candidates may have been better at answering traditional exam questions with no notes. • **Students can become addicted to open-notes exams.** This sometimes means that they lose the skills of preparing for traditional unseen exams, and don't invest enough in memorising what may be needed for those exams. • **Extra desk space is needed, just as for open-book exams.** The intended learning outcome is not that students should demonstrate the ability to manage

Table 4 continued

Advantages	Disadvantages
• **You can write shorter questions.** When it is up to the students to ensure that they have with them important information or data, you don't have to put so much into the questions themselves.	a lot of pieces of paper on a small desk without any falling off!

Many of the suggestions given in the previous two sections continue to apply to designing open-notes exams. However, the further considerations may help you to put open-notes exams to good use.

1 **Think of giving a topic menu in advance.** This can save candidates from trying to prepare open notes on everything they have learned about your topic. It does, of course, also mean that you are letting them off the hook regarding trying to learn some of the things that you *don't* include in your menu.

2 **Consider having an inspection process.** For example, let it be known that your or your colleagues will be keeping an eye on the range and content of the open notes, or even that they may be temporarily retained after the exam.

3 **Consider placing a limit on the notes allowed.** For example, students attending a series of seminars could be permitted one large (specified) index card per seminar on which to make notes, and only these cards would then be allowed to be used as open notes.

13

Structured exams

Structured exams include multiple-choice exams and several other types of formats in which students are not required to write 'full' answers, but have to make true–false decisions, or identify reasons to support assertions, or fill in blanks or complete statements, and so on. It is of course possible to design mixed exams combining free-response traditional questions with structured ones. In the following discussion, we will concentrate on the benefits and drawbacks of multiple-choice questions. Many of the same points also apply at least in part to other types of structured exam questions, such as true–false, short-answer and sequencing questions.

Table 5 Advantages and disadvantages of assessment via structured exams

Advantages	Disadvantages
• **Reliability can be excellent.** Because of the structure, consistency can be assured.	• **The guess factor.** Students can often gain marks by lucky guesses rather than correct decisions.
• **Validity can also be excellent.** Where the best way to assess students' knowledge is to get them to make decisions, structured exams can test this decision-making directly, without any interference from such things as speed of handwriting, or difficulties with spelling, grammar or punctuation.	• **Designing structured questions takes time and skill.** It is harder to design good multiple-choice questions than it is to write traditional open-ended questions. In particular, it can be difficult to think of the last distractor or to make it look sufficiently plausible. It is sometimes difficult to prevent the correct answer or best option standing out as being the one to choose.
• **Greater syllabus coverage:** it is possible, in a limited time, to test students' understanding of a much greater cross-section of a syllabus than could be done in the same time by getting students to write in detail about a few parts of the syllabus.	• **The 'best' option needs to definitely be the best!** Sometimes in multiple-choice questions, the most able candidates can see something wrong with what is supposed to be the 'best' option, and end up losing marks by not choosing it.
• **Multiple-choice exams test how fast students think,** rather than how fast	

Table 5 continued

Advantages	Disadvantages
they write. The level of their thinking depends on how skilled the question-setters have been.	• **Black and white or shades of grey?** While it is straightforward enough to reward students with marks for correct choices (with zero marks for choosing distractors), it is more difficult to handle subjects where there is a 'best' option and a 'next-best' one, and so on.
• **Students waste less time.** Questions can already show, for example, formulae, definitions, equations and statements (correct and wrong), and students can be asked to select the correct one without having to provide it for themselves.	
• **Staff time and energy are saved.** With optical mark readers, it is possible to mark paper-based multiple choice exams very cost-effectively, and avoid the tedium and subjectivity that affect the marking of traditional exams.	• **Where multiple-choice exams are being set on computers, check that the tests are secure.** Students can be ingenious at getting into computer files that are intended to be secret!
• **Computer-based tests can save even more time.** As well as processing all of the scores, computer software can work out how each question performs, calculating the discrimination index and facility value of each question. This allows the questions that work well as testing devices to be identified, and selected for future exams.	• **The danger of impersonators?** The fact that exams composed entirely of multiple-choice questions do not require students to give any evidence of their handwriting increases the risk of substitution of candidates. You may need to cross-check photo identification with candidate numbers.
• **Testing higher-level skills?** Multiple-choice exams can move the emphasis away from memory and towards the ability to interpret information and make good decisions.	• **Some special needs may be involved.** Students with some kinds of disability (particularly impairments associated with vision) may find multiple-choice questions hard, when choosing the best option from four or five similar-looking responses. They could need extra time and rehearsal.
	• **Some believe that only lower cognitive skills can be tested.** High-level skills can, however, be tested effectively using a range of question types going far beyond 'choose one answer from five', and more attention needs to be given to the design of such testing to build on these.

Designing multiple-choice exams

Multiple choice is one of the most popular formats for structured testing, and is now widely used in many areas of education, and in particular disciplines has been developed very thoroughly. However, when multiple-choice questions are used for exams rather than just for self-assessment, feedback or diagnostic testing, much more care needs to be taken regarding the design and validation of the questions. The following suggestions may help you to devise effective multiple-choice exams.

1 **Check the performance of each question with large numbers of students before including it in an exam.** The most suitable questions are those that discriminate between the able and the less able candidates. There are statistical packages that can help you work out the 'facility value' of questions (how easy or difficult they are) and the 'discrimination index' of questions (how well they separate the best candidates from the rest). Ideally, all questions should have been through trialling with hundreds of students before the most suitable of them are used in a formal exam.

2 **Start the exam with some relatively straightforward questions.** This helps anxious candidates to get into their stride, and is better than having such candidates thrown into a panic by an early tricky question.

3 **Make the most of the opportunity to give students quick feedback.** An advantage of multiple-choice exams is that it is perfectly possible to arrange not only that students get their scores very quickly, but also that they receive detailed feedback reminding them of their correct decisions and explaining why other decisions were incorrect.

4 **Make sure that candidates aren't going to be getting questions right for the wrong reasons.** Look for any give-aways in the keys or context of the questions. During trialling, if too many students get a question right, it could be that the question is too easy to serve a useful purpose in testing, or something may be giving away the correct option to choose.

5 **Watch out for cases where the best candidates choose a distractor.** This usually happens when they can see something wrong with the option that is supposed to be undeniably correct, or 'best'. This can be done manually by scanning the responses from a large group of students, if you have prior knowledge of who the most able students are. Computer software can normally help by identifying all students who have got a particular question wrong, and can be programmed to search for candidates with a high overall score who get these particular questions wrong.

6 **Help candidates to develop their skills at tackling multiple-choice exams.** Give candidates past papers to practise on, and provide advice on the most effective techniques for tackling this form of exam. This can provide them with valuable formative feedback prior to summative assessments.

7 **Decide whether you really want an against-the-clock exam.** Find out how long candidates take on average. With a timed exam, there is some tendency for candidates to rush their decision-making, and even if they have plenty of time left over, they are still left with a hangover legacy of questions where they made wrong decisions.

8   **Make sure that distractors are plausible.** If no one is selecting a given distractor, it is serving no useful purpose. Distractors need to represent anticipated errors in students' knowledge or understanding.

9   **Try to avoid overlap between questions.** If one question helps students successfully to answer further questions, the possibility increases of students picking the right options for the wrong reasons.

10 **Avoid options such as 'none of the above' or 'all of the above'.** These options are a let-out for students who find it hard to decide between the other alternatives, and are often chosen by weaker students in surface-thinking mode. Also, it is surprisingly rare for such options to be in fact the correct one, and test-wise candidates will already have guessed this. To complicate matters, the best students will sometimes spot weaknesses with the option that is intended to be correct, and select 'none of these' because of this.

11 **Write feedback responses to each option.** Where possible, it is useful to be able to explain to students selecting the correct (or best) option exactly *why* their selection is right. It is even more useful to be able to explain to students selecting the wrong (or less good) options exactly what may be wrong with their understanding. When multiple-choice questions are computer marked, it is a simple further step to get the computer to print out feedback responses to each student. This practice can equally be applied to formative multiple-choice tests and to formal multiple-choice exams. Furthermore, the availability of feedback responses to each decision students make lends itself to extending the use of such questions in computer-based learning packages, and even computer-managed exams.

12 **Remember that students can still guess.** The marking scheme needs to take into account the fact that students will score some marks by pure luck! Computer-based assessment software can help to ensure that different marks are awarded for different distractors, to ensure at least that not every guess is equally weighted! Otherwise, if most of the questions are, for example, four-option ones, the average mark that would be scored by someone choosing options randomly would be 25 per cent, so the real range lies between this and 100 per cent. It is important that people are indeed allowed to get 100 per cent in such structured exams, and that this does not cause any problems when the marks are blended with more traditional exam formats in which written answers in some subjects still attract marks only in the seventies even when they're reckoned to be first-class answers.

13 **Ensure that students are well practised at handling multiple-choice questions.** Answering such questions well is a skill in its own right, just as is writing open answers well. We need to ensure that students are sufficiently

practised so that multiple-choice exams measure their understanding and not just their technique.

14 **Look at a range of published multiple-choice questions.** For example, in the United Kingdom, several Open University courses have multiple-choice assignment questions, as well as multiple-choice exams. You may be surprised at how sophisticated such questions can be, and may gain many ideas that you can build into your own question design.

15 **Gradually build up a large bank of questions.** This is best done by collaborating with colleagues and pooling questions that are found to be working well. It then becomes possible to compose a multiple-choice exam by selecting from the bank of questions. If the bank becomes large enough, it can even be good practice to publish the whole collection and allow students to practise with it.

16 **When you've got a large bank of questions, there is the possibility of on-demand exams.** Students can then take a multiple-choice test with a random selection of questions from the bank at any time during their studies, and 'pass' the component involved as soon as they are able to demonstrate their competence with the questions.

17 **Look for ways of making marking quick and easy.** When large numbers of candidates are involved, you should use optical mark-reading techniques or computer-aided testing formats. When designing question papers the answers to which will be read by optical mark-reading, discuss with your technical colleagues how to make this straightforward. For example, don't use shadowed boxes for candidates to mark into, or place boxes too closely together on the paper.

18 **Get some colleagues to take your exam.** They may be surprised at things they find that they did not know, and they may give you some surprises too about what you *thought* were cut-and-dried questions.

14

Vivas – oral exams

Viva voce exams have long been used to add to or consolidate the results of other forms of assessment. In many countries, oral exams of one kind or another play a much more important part in higher education assessment than in the United Kingdom. Such exams normally take the form of a 'defence' of an argument, where students are interrogated by one or more examiners about selected parts of work they have had assessed in other ways. Such exams are often used to make decisions about the classification of degree candidates whose work straddles borderlines.

Table 6 Advantages and disadvantages of assessment via vivas

Advantages	Disadvantages
• **Authenticity is tested directly – and indeed quickly.** Vivas are useful checks on the ownership of evidence. It is relatively easy to use a viva to ensure that students are familiar with things that other forms of assessment seem to indicate they have learned well. • **Vivas seem useful when searching for particular things.** For example, vivas have long been used to help make decisions about borderline cases in degree classifications, particularly when the written work or exam performance has for some reason fallen below what might have been expected for particular candidates. • **Candidates may be examined fairly.** With a well-constructed agenda for a viva, a series of candidates may be asked the same questions, and their responses compared and evaluated.	• **Some candidates never show themselves well in vivas.** Cultural and individual differences can result in some candidates underperforming when asked questions by experts and figures of authority. • **The agenda may 'leak'.** When the same series of questions is being posed to a succession of students, it is quite difficult to ensure that candidates who have already been examined aren't able to communicate with friends whose turn is still to come. • **You need to beware of level drift.** It is dangerously easy for your questions to become gradually tougher as you work your way through all the candidates. • **The actual agenda covered by a viva is usually narrow.** Vivas are seldom good as measures of how well students have

Table 6 continued

Advantages	Disadvantages
• **Vivas give useful practice for interviews for employment.** Sadly, for most vivas what is at stake is more serious than a possible appointment, so it is worth considering using vivas more widely but less formally to allow students to develop the appropriate skills without too much depending on their performance.	learned and understood large parts of the syllabus. • **Vivas cannot be anonymous!** Assessors assessing viva performance can be influenced by what they already know about the students' work. However, it is possible to use assessors who don't know the students at all, or to include such assessors in a viva panel.

Designing and implementing oral exams

1   **Remind yourself what the viva is for.** Purposes vary, but it is important to be clear about it at the outset. For example, the agenda could include one or more of the following: confirming that the candidates did indeed do the work represented in their dissertations; probing whether a poor examination result was an uncharacteristic slip; or checking on whether students' understanding of the subject reached acceptable levels.

2   **Prepare your students for vivas.** Explain to them what a viva is, and what they will normally be expected to do. It helps to give them opportunities to practise. Much of this they can do on their own or in pairs, but they will need you to start them off on the right lines, and to check now and then that their practice sessions are realistic.

3   **Think about the room layout.** Sitting the candidate on a hard seat while you and your fellow assessors sit face-on behind a large table is guaranteed to make the candidate tremble! If possible, sit beside or close to the candidate, without their being able to see your notes. Where appropriate, provide students with a table on which to put any papers they may have with them.

4   **Prepare yourself for vivas!** Normally, if you're a principal player at a viva, you will have read the student's work in some detail. It helps if you come to the viva armed with a list of questions you may ask. You don't have to ask all of them, but it helps to have some ready! Normally, you may need to have a pre-viva discussion with other members of the examining panel, and you need to be seen to have done your homework. Use Post-it™ notes in the text of scripts to help you to keep tabs on exactly where your queries or discussion points are located.

5   **Prepare the agenda in advance, and with colleagues.** It is dangerously easy (and unfair to students) for the agenda to develop during a series of

interviews with different students. Prepare and use a checklist or pro forma to keep records. Memory is not sufficient, and can be unreliable, especially when different examiners conducting a viva have different agendas.

6   **Do your best to put the candidate at ease.** Students find vivas very stressful, and it improves their confidence and fluency if they are greeted cheerily and made welcome at the start of a viva.

7   **When vivas are a formality, indicate this.** When students have done well on the written side of their work and it's fairly certain that they will pass, it helps to give a strong hint about this straight away. It puts students at ease, and makes for a more interesting and relaxed viva.

8   **Ensure there are no surprises.** Share the agenda with each candidate and clarify the processes to be used. You are likely to get more out of candidates this way.

9   **Ask open questions that enable students to give full and articulate answers.** Try to avoid questions that lead to minimal or 'yes/no' replies.

10 **Let students do most of the talking.** The role of an examiner in a viva is to provoke thought and prompt candidates into speaking fluently about the work or topics under discussion, and to spark off an intellectual dialogue. It is not to harangue, carp or demonstrate the examiner's intelligence, or to trick candidates!

11 **Prepare to be able to debrief well.** Write your own notes during each viva. If you are dealing with a series of such events, it can become difficult to remember each feedback point that you want to give to each student. Vivas can be very useful learning experiences, but much of the experience can be lost if time is not set aside for a debriefing. Such debriefing is particularly useful when students will encounter vivas again.

12 **When debriefing, ask students for their opinions first.** This can spare them the embarrassment of having you telling them about failings they already know they have. You may also find useful food for thought when students tell you about aspects of the vivas that you were unaware of yourself.

13 **Be sensitive.** Vivas can be traumatic for students, and they may have put much time and effort into preparing for them. Choose words carefully particularly when giving feedback on aspects that were unsuccessful.

14 **Be specific.** Students will naturally want to have feedback on details of things they did particularly well. As far as you can, make sure you can find something positive to say even when overall performance was not good.

15 **Consider recording practice vivas on video.** This is particularly worthwhile when one of your main aims is to prepare students for more important vivas to follow. Simply allowing students to borrow the recordings and look at them in the comfort of privacy can provide students with useful deep reflection on their performance. It is sometimes more comfortable to view the recordings in the atmosphere of a supportive student group.

16 **Run a role-play afterwards.** Ask students to play both examiners and candidates, and bring to life some of the issues they encountered in their vivas. This can allow other students observing the role-play to think about aspects they did not experience themselves.

17 **Plan for the next step.** Get students to discuss strategies for preparing for their next viva, and ask groups of students to make lists of 'dos and don'ts' to bear in mind next time.

18 **Get students to produce a guidance booklet about preparing for vivas and taking part in them.** This may be useful for future students, but is equally valuable to the students making it, as a way of getting them to consolidate their reflections on their own experience.

15

Some other kinds of examination

The discussion in this chapter so far has addressed only some of the possibilities. There are various alternative forms of exam, some now widely used, that achieve both authenticity (meaning that we know the exam is the work of the candidate) and high levels of validity and reliability. The following descriptions are just a start; you may already be using these or more adventurous varieties of exam.

1   **Objective structured clinical exams (OSCEs).** These are used widely in medical education, and have been described as 'circuit training for doctors'. There is still an 'exam room', but this is full of 'assessment stations' that candidates visit in turn and do their stuff. For example, at one they may interpret some X-rays, at another they may make a diagnosis from other medical records of a patient, and at another they may interview a patient (actually, it's usually an *actor* as patients can't usually be found who tell exactly the same story to successive doctor-candidates!). Such exams are very high on validity: they measure what doctors need to be able to do. They are often easier to 'mark' than a traditional written exam (and not just because doctors' handwriting is legendarily bad!). But they do take a lot of planning.

2   **In-tray exams.** These are used in many subject areas, including business, and ward management for hospital staff. Take the latter. They go to their exam desks at 09.30, but there are no questions, just a pile of data – the patients presently in the ward, the staff on duty, the staff on call, and so on. The candidates have perhaps 20 minutes simply to make sense of the data provided to them; they can scribble on the data sheets, stick Post-it™ notes to them, and so on. But at 09.50 a slip of paper appears on each desk with (for example) the following information:

> Accident at the airport. The following three cases are on their way to you by ambulance – the first will arrive in less than 10 minutes. What will you do? How will you prepare for them? Who will you move? Who will you call? What will you have set up for each of the three?

Candidates hand in their answers to these questions by (say) 10.10, and are given the next stage of their task.

Exams of this sort are again very high in validity: they measure what candidates will be expected to be able to do in practice. Such exams depend not on essay-writing skills, but on decision-making and clear communication of those decisions to the people affected by them. Such exams take a lot of planning, but are quick – and very fair – to mark.

3   **Take-away exams.** Candidates arrive at the exam room say at 09.30, pick up the question or task, and go away. They go to the library, or to their study-bedroom, or onto the Internet, or wherever they wish. They talk to anyone they wish, they phone a friend, or whatever. At 17.00 (say) they bring back their answer to the question and hand it in. Such exams are very high on validity – this is how the real world works. There is, of course, a problem with authenticity – but this too is how the real world works. If you set take-away papers over an extended period (for example, over a weekend or a week), be sensitive to the extra demands these will make on those candidates with caring responsibilities.

4   **Computer-adaptive testing.** This is a form of computer-based multiple-choice testing – but an 'intelligent' adaptation. For example, there is a large bank of multiple-choice questions on the system, each with known facility value (easy to hard) and each with known discrimination index (how well it sorts out the most able from the least able candidates). The computer fires a particular question at a candidate. If the candidate gets it right, it fires a slightly harder one, and so on. If the candidate gets it wrong, the computer fires a slightly easier question, and so on. The computer is programmed to find out each candidate's 'level' using only as many questions as it takes to do so reliably. Such testing has been developed best in the medical education field to date, where it has been shown to be very reliable when used alongside more traditional methods of judging candidates.

Chapter 3

Specific assessment formats

16   Essays
17   Reviews and annotated bibliographies
18   Reports
19   Practical work
20   Portfolios
21   Presentations
22   Assessing performances
23   Student projects
24   Poster displays and exhibitions
25   Dissertations and theses
26   Work-based learning

16

Essays

In some subjects, assessment is dominated by essay-writing. Traditional (and open-book) exams often require students to write essays. Assessed coursework too often takes the form of essays. It is well known that essay-answers tend to be harder to mark, and more time-consuming to assess, than answers to quantitative or numerical questions. There are still some useful functions to be served by including some essay questions in exams, however.

Table 7 Advantages and disadvantages of assessment via essay examination questions

Advantages	Disadvantages
• **Familiarity.** Students may have had a lot of practice at writing essays, so know what to do to get good marks in them, whereas may need training and rehearsal to develop skills relevant to other forms of assessment. Staff often find the format reassuringly familiar too, and you won't usually need to explain the use of essays to external examiners. • **Essays allow for student individuality and expression.** They are a medium in which the 'best' students can distinguish themselves. This means, however, that the marking criteria for essays must be flexible enough to be able to reward student individuality fairly. • **Essays can reflect the depth of student learning.** Writing freely about a topic is a process that demonstrates understanding and grasp of the material involved.	• **Validity is often compromised.** Essay-writing is very much an art in itself. Students from some backgrounds are disadvantaged regarding essay-writing skills as they have simply never been coached in how to write essays well. For example, a strong beginning, a coherent and logical middle, and a firm and decisive conclusion combine to make up the hallmarks of a good essay. The danger becomes that when essays are overused in assessment strategies, the presence of these hallmarks is measured time and time again, and students who happen to have perfected the art of delivering these hallmarks are repeatedly rewarded irrespective of any other strengths and weaknesses they may have. • **Essays take a great deal of time to mark objectively.** Even with well-thought-out assessment criteria, it is not unusual for markers to need to work back

Table 7 continued

Advantages	Disadvantages
• **Essay-writing is a measure of students' written style.** It is useful to include good written communication somewhere in the overall assessment strategy. The danger of students in science disciplines missing out on the development of such skills is becoming increasingly recognised.	through the first dozen or so of the essays they have already marked, as they become aware of the things that the best students are doing with the questions, and the difficulties experienced by other students.
• **Essays enable students to demonstrate coherence.** They can be evidence of students' abilities to construct fluent and logical arguments.	• **'Halo effects' are significant.** If the last essay answer you marked was an excellent one, you may tend to approach the next one with greater expectations, and be more severe in your assessment decisions based upon it.
• **Synopsis.** Essays can provide opportunities for students to bring together different strands of their thinking into a single argument.	• **Essays take time to write (whether as coursework or in exams).** This means that assessment based on essay-writing necessarily is restricted regarding the amount of the syllabus that is covered directly. There may remain large untested tracts of syllabus.
	• **'Write down everything you know about . . .'** Students often see an essay title as the starting pistol to regurgitate all they know on a topic – and too often they find that this strategy seems to be rewarded by marks or grades.
	• **'Award the essay the mark or grade I first thought of!'** Essays are demonstrably the form of assessment in which the dangers of subjective marking are greatest. Essay-marking exercises at workshops on assessment show marked differences between the mark or grade that different assessors award the same essay – even when equipped with clear sets of assessment criteria.

Setting and using essay-type questions

Most of the suggestions given earlier about writing traditional exam questions continue to apply – whether essays are to be used as assessed coursework or as exam questions. Some further suggestions are given here.

1   **Help students to see exactly how essays are marked.** Alert students to the credit they gain from good structure and style. One of the best ways of doing this is to involve classes of students in looking at examples of past

(good, bad and indifferent) essays and applying assessment criteria. This can be followed by involving students in peer assessment of each other's essays.

2 **Don't leave students to guess the real agenda.** Some essay questions are so open ended that it is hard for students to work out exactly what is being sought. The authors of such questions will defend their questions by saying, 'Well, it's important to find the students who know what to do in such circumstances', but the fact remains that it is an aspect of study technique that is being rewarded, rather than mastery of the learning involved in answering the question.

3 **Subdivide essay questions into several parts, each with marks publicly allocated.** This helps to prevent students from straying so far off the point that they lose too many of the marks that they could have scored.

4 **Give word limits.** Even in exams, it can be useful to suggest to students that an essay answer should lie between (for example) 800 and 1,200 words, say for a 30-minute question, and so on. This helps to avoid the quantity versus quality issue, which leads some students into simply trying to write a lot, rather than thinking deeply about what they are writing – and it also helps reduce the time it takes to mark the essays.

5 **Help students to develop the skills required to plan the content for essays.** This is particularly important in those disciplines in which students will be more accustomed to handling structured questions and problems. The danger then is that students tackling essay questions in exams spend far too long on them, and penalise themselves regarding time for the rest of the examination. One of the best – and most time-effective – ways of helping students to become better at handling essay questions is to set class or coursework tasks that require students to prepare essay plans rather than fully finished masterpieces. A concept map or diagram can show a great deal about the eventual 'worth' of students' essays, and can avoid distraction by the elements of style and structure. Students can put together maybe half a dozen essay plans in the time it would take them to complete one essay, and making the plans involves far more pay-off per unit time in thinking and learning.

6 **Don't assess using essays too often.** Any form of assessment advantages those students who happen to be skilled at delivering what is being measured. This applies to essays too, and there is a significant danger that those students who happen to become good at planning and writing essays continue to be advantaged time and time again.

7 **Have a clear, well-structured marking scheme for each essay question.** This can save a lot of time when marking, and can help guarantee that students' answers are assessed fairly and consistently.

8   **Don't assume that longer equals better.** It is often harder for students to write succinctly than just to ramble on. However, students need to be briefed on how best we want them to develop their art in writing briefly.

9   **Consider involving students in peer-assessing some essays or essay plans.** This helps them to put their own efforts into perspective, and to learn things to emulate (and things to avoid!) by seeing how other students go about devising essays.

10 **Help students to improve their technique through feedback.** Consider the range of approaches you can use to give students useful feedback on their essays, including statement banks, assignment return sheets and email messages, and try to minimise the time you spend writing similar feedback comments onto different students' essays.

11 **Use some class time to get students to brainstorm titles for essays.** This helps them to think about the standard they could anticipate for essay questions in forthcoming exams, and gives them topic areas to base their practice on.

17

Reviews and annotated bibliographies

Anyone who reviews books or articles for journals or magazines will confirm that there's no better way of making oneself look deeply into a book or article than to be charged with the task of writing a review of it! Getting students to write reviews is therefore a logical way of causing them to interact in depth with the information they review. One way of getting students to review a lot of material at once is to ask them to produce annotated bibliographies on a topic area, and to use these as assessment artefacts.

Table 8 Advantages and disadvantages of assessment via student-produced annotated bibliographies

Advantages	Disadvantages
• **Validity can be high.** Reviewing and searching the literature are important skills, and can be measured quite directly.	• **Reviews are necessarily quite individual.** For reviews to lend themselves to assessment, it is important that the task should be delineated quite firmly. This may go against the open-ended approach to reviewing that we may wish students to develop.
• **Reviewing is an active process.** Reviewing material gives students a task to do that focuses their thinking and helps them avoid reading passively, or writing the content out in 'transcribing' mode.	
	• **There may not be sufficient books and journals available.** With large numbers of students and limited library resources, students may find it difficult or impossible to get adequate access to the materials we want them to review. This could end up as grounds for appeal against assessment decisions, if students felt that they had been disadvantaged.
• **Reviews are useful for revision.** When students have reviewed material, the reviews are useful learning tools in their own right, and may spare students from having to wade through the material on subsequent revision.	
• **Reviewing involves important cognitive processes.** When students are required to review material from different sources critically, they are necessarily engaged in higher-level	• **Reviewing individually can be lonely.** Reviewing a range of resources is often best done as a group task rather than an individual one, maximising the benefits that students derive from discussion and

Table 8 continued

Advantages	Disadvantages
skills of comparing, contrasting and evaluating – far beyond passive reading. • **Reviewing other papers and articles is useful practice for research writing.** Students who will move on to research can benefit from the training involved in writing reviews, and gain skills in communicating their conclusions coherently. • **Reviewing helps students to develop critical skills.** Getting students to compare and contrast chosen sources helps them think more deeply about the subject matter involved. • **Compiling annotated bibliographies is a way of requiring students to survey a considerable amount of material.** It also helps them to reduce a large field to a manageable body of notes and references.	debate. It then becomes more difficult to assess individual contributions to such reviews. • **Books and other sources are different.** If you ask students to review a range of resources, some may be harder to understand than others. Similarly, some may be more central to the course programme than others.

Setting assessed review tasks

1   **Promote variety.** Ask students to select their own subject for research, and give them a wide range of topics to choose from.

2   **Prompt awareness of audience.** Ask students to write reviews of different kinds of publication (learned journal, subject magazine, next year's students, student newsletter, and so on), so that they become aware of the differences in tone and style of writing that are appropriate for different audiences.

3   **Get students to assess existing reviews.** For example, issue students with a selection of existing reviews and ask them to identify features of the best samples, and faults of the worst ones.

4   **Help students to see that reviewing is not just a matter of summarising what everyone has said.** You only have to look at book reviews in journals to see how some reviewers make up their contributions by summarising the contents pages of the material that they are reviewing. This is not a high-level intellectual activity; the best reviews also involve evaluation.

5   **Decide about credit to be awarded to 'search' tasks.** It is useful to get students both to locate all relevant major resources addressing a field, and

to prioritise (for example) the most important or most relevant half-dozen sources.

6   **Consider limiting the parameters.** If you get students to do a short comparative review of two or three important sources, it can be easier (and fairer) to assess the results than it would be if the reviews were done without any restrictions. When such focused review tasks are coupled with a general search, it is possible to measure information retrieval skills as well as the higher-level 'compare and contrast' skills, without the agenda for the latter remaining too wide for objective assessment.

7   **Set a tight word-limit for the review.** Writing a good short review is more demanding than writing a long review. When students' reviews are of equal length, it becomes easier to distinguish the relative quality of their work. However, brief students on how to draft and redraft their work, to ensure the quality of short reviews. Make sure that students don't adopt the 'stop when you've written a thousand words' approach.

8   **Think about combining collaborative and individual work.** For example, suggest that groups of students do a search collaboratively and identify the most relevant sources together. Then suggest they write individual reviews of different sources. Finally, consider asking them to share their reviews, then write individual comments comparing and contrasting the sources.

9   **Ask students to look at the same texts, but give them different focuses.** For example, students could look at a series of articles on pollution and write different reviews of them aimed to be separately useful to conservationists, parents, individualists and general consumers.

10 **Encourage qualitative judgement.** Prompt students to write not only on what a book or article is about, but also about how effective it is in providing convincing arguments, and how well it is expressed.

11 **Involve your library or information services staff.** It's a mean trick to send off large groups of students to rampage through the library without giving notice to the staff there of what you are doing. Discussing your plans with your faculty librarians, for example, gives them a chance to be prepared, and gives opportunities for them to make suggestions and give advice to you on the nature of the task before you give it to students.

12 **Explore the possibility of involving library staff in the assessment.** Library staff may be willing and able to assess annotated bibliographies and reviews in parallel with yourself, or may be willing to provide additional feedback comments to students.

13   **Think hard about resource availability.** Make sure that there won't be severe log-jams with lots of students chasing particular library resources. Widen the range of suggested resources. Consider arranging with library staff that any books that will be in heavy demand are classified as 'reference only' stock for a specified period, so that they can remain in the library rather than disappearing on loan.

14   **Consider setting annotated bibliographies as formative group tasks.** This can encourage students to collaborate productively in future information-seeking tasks, and can reduce the drudgery sometimes experienced in tasks such as literature searching. Giving feedback on the reviews can be sufficiently valuable to students to make it unnecessary to couple the task with formal assessment.

15   **Consider making the final product 'publishable'.** Aim to compile collections of the best reviews and annotated bibliographies, for example to use in next year's course handbook, or as the basis of an assessed task for next year's students.

18

Reports

Assessed reports make up at least part of the coursework component of many courses. Report-writing is one of the most problematic study-skills areas in which to work out how and what to advise students to do to develop their approaches. The format, layout, style and nature of an acceptable report vary greatly from one discipline to another, and even from one assessor to another in the same discipline. The most common kinds of report that many students write are those associated with their practical work, laboratory work or fieldwork. Several of the suggestions offered in this section relate particularly to report-writing in science and engineering disciplines, but can readily be extended to other subject areas.

Table 9 Advantages and disadvantages of assessment via students' reports

Advantages	Disadvantages
• **Report-writing is a skill relevant to many jobs.** In many careers and professional areas, the ability to put together a convincing and precise report is useful. Report-writing can therefore provide a medium whereby specific skills relevant to professional activity can be addressed.	• **Collaboration can be difficult to detect.** For example, with laboratory work there may be a black market in old reports! Also, when students are working in pairs or groups in practical work, it can be difficult to set the boundaries between collaborative work and individual interpretation of results.
• **Reports can be the end product of useful learning activities.** For example, the task of writing reports can involve students in research, practical work, analysis of data, comparing measured findings with literature values, prioritising, and many other useful processes. Sometimes these processes are hard or impossible to assess directly, and reports provide secondary evidence that they have been involved successfully (or not).	• **Report-writing can take a lot of student time.** When reports are assessed and count towards final grades, there is the danger that students spend too much time writing them at the expense of getting to grips with their subject matter in a way that will ensure that they succeed in other forms of assessment such as exams.
	• **Report-marking can take a lot of staff time.** With increased numbers of students, it becomes more difficult to find

Table 9 continued

Advantages	Disadvantages
• **Report-writing can allow students to display their talents.** The fact that students can have more control when they write reports than when they answer exam questions allows students to display their individual strengths.	the time to mark piles of reports and to maintain the quality and quantity of feedback given to students about their work. • **Report-writing can dwindle into drudgery.** Writing too many lab reports in the same kind of structure and format, for example, can become repetitive and dull.

Designing assessed report-writing

1 **Give clear guidance regarding the format of reports.** For example, issue a sheet listing principal generic section headings, with a short description of the purpose and nature of each main section in a typical report. Remind students, when necessary, of the importance of this guidance in your ongoing feedback on their reports.

2 **Get students to assess subjectively some past reports.** Issue students with copies of some good, bad and indifferent reports and ask them to mark them independently, simply giving each example an impression mark. Then facilitate a discussion in which students explain why they allocated the marks in the ways they did.

3 **Get students to assess objectively some past reports.** Issue groups of students with good, bad and indifferent reports, along with a sheet listing assessment criteria and a mark scheme. Ask each group to assess the reports, then initiate discussions and comparisons between groups.

4 **Make explicit the assessment criteria for reports.** Help students to see the balance between the marks associated with the structure of their reports, and those given to the content and the level of critical thinking and analysis.

5 **Ask students for full reports less often.** For example, if during a course students tackle eight pieces of work involving report-writing, ask students to write full reports for only two of these, and summary or 'short-form' or 'memorandum' reports for the remaining assignments. These shorter reports can be structured in note form or as a set of bullet points, yet still show much evidence of the thinking and analysis that students have done.

6 **Accommodate collaboration.** One way round the problems of collaboration is to develop approaches whereby students are required to prepare

reports in groups – which is often closer to situations encountered in real life than preparing them individually is.

7   **Involve students in assessing each other's reports.** When marks for reports 'count' significantly, it may be desirable to moderate student peer assessment in one way or another, but probably the greatest benefit of peer assessment is that students gain a good deal more feedback about their work than hard-pressed staff are able to provide. It is far quicker to moderate student peer assessment than to mark all the reports from scratch.

8   **Consider asking students to write (or word-process) some reports onto pre-prepared pro formas.** This can help where there are significant 'given' elements such as equipment and methodology. You can then concentrate on assessing the important parts of their writing – for example, interpretation of data.

9   **Consider getting students to do 'live' laboratory reports, on computers placed alongside the lab equipment.** You can then monitor their individual activity and reduce the risk of their falling behind in their report-writing post hoc. Many universities now enable students to write up their reports straight into a word processor alongside the laboratory bench, using a report template on disk. Such reports can be handed in immediately at the end of the laboratory session, or submitted online, and then marked and returned promptly.

10 **Publish clear deadlines for the submission of successive reports.** For example, in the case of practical work, allow only one or two weeks after the laboratory session. It is kinder to students to get them to write up early, rather than allow them to accumulate a backlog of report-writing, which can interfere (for example) with their revision for exams.

11 **Prepare a standard assessment/feedback grid to return to students with marked reports.** Include criteria and marks associated with (for example) the quality of data, observations, calculations, conclusions, references and verdicts.

12 **Start students thinking even before the practical work.** For example, allocate practical work in advance of laboratory sessions and include some assessed pre-laboratory preparation as a prelude to the eventual report. One way of doing this is to pose half a dozen short-answer questions for students to complete before starting a piece of laboratory work. This helps students know what they are doing, rather than follow instructions blindly. It also avoids wasting time spent at the start of a laboratory session working out only then which students are to undertake each experiment.

13 **Include in examinations some questions linked closely to practical work or fieldwork.** For example, tell students that two exam questions will be based on work they will have done outside the lecture room. This helps to ensure that practical work and associated reports don't get forgotten when students start revising for exams.

14 **Get students to design exam questions based on the work covered by their reports.** Set groups of students this task. Allocate some marks for the creativity of their questions. When this is done over several years, the products could be turned into a bank of questions that could be placed on computer for students to consult as they prepare for exams.

19

Practical work

Many areas of study involve practical work, but it is often much more difficult to assess such work in its own right; assessing reports of practical work may involve measuring the quality only of the end product of the practical work, and not of the work itself. The following discussion attempts to help you to think of ways of addressing the assessment of the practical work itself.

Table 10 Advantages and disadvantages of assessment via practical work

Advantages	Disadvantages
• **Practical work is really important in some disciplines.** In many areas of the physical sciences, for example, practical skills are just as important as theoretical competences. Students proceeding to research or industry will be expected to have acquired a wide range of practical skills.	• **It is often difficult to assess practical work in its own right.** It is usually much easier to assess the end-point of practical work, rather than the processes and skills involved in their own right.
• **Employers may need to know how good students' practical skills are (and not just how good their reports are).** It is therefore useful to reserve part of our overall assessment for practical skills themselves, and not just the final written products of practical work.	• **It can be difficult to agree on assessment criteria for practical skills.** There may be several ways of performing a task well, requiring a range of alternative assessment criteria.
• **Practical work is learning by doing.** Increasing the significance of practical work by attaching assessment to it helps students approach such work more earnestly and critically.	• **Students may be inhibited when someone is observing their performance.** When one is doing laboratory work, for example, it can be very distracting to be watched! Similar considerations apply to practical exercises such as interviewing, counselling, advising, and other 'soft skills' that are part of the agenda of many courses.

Assessing practical work: questions and suggestions

This time we're posing questions rather than just giving suggestions. Practical work varies a lot between different disciplines, and it is important to address a number of questions about the nature and context of practical work, the answers to which help to clarify how best to go about assessing such work. So first the questions, then some suggestions.

1   **What exactly are the practical skills we wish to assess?** These may include a vast range of important skills, from deftness in assembling complex glassware in a chemistry laboratory to precision and speed in using a scalpel on the operating table. It is important that students know the relative importance of each skill.

2   **Why do we need to measure practical skills?** The credibility of our courses sometimes depends on what students can do when they enter employment. It is often said by employers that students are very knowledgeable, but not necessarily competent in practical tasks.

3   **Where is the best place to try to measure these skills?** Sometimes practical skills can be measured in places such as laboratories or workshops. For other skills, students may need to be working in real-life situations.

4   **When is the best time to measure practical skills?** When practical skills are vitally important, it is probably best to start measuring them very early on in a course, so that any students showing alarming problems with them can be appropriately advised or redirected.

5   **Who is in the best position to measure practical skills?** For many practical skills, the only valid way of measuring them involves someone doing detailed observations while students demonstrate the skills involved. This can be very time-consuming if it has to be done by staff, and also can feel very threatening to students. In the workplace, practical skills can be assessed by employers or placement supervisors, but they are likely to need thorough briefing and training to play this part in assessing students' work.

6   **Is it necessary to establish minimum acceptable standards?** In many jobs it is quite essential that everyone practising does so with a high level of skill (for example, surgery!). In other situations, it is possible to agree on a reasonable level of skills, and for this to be safe enough (for example, teaching!).

7   **How much should practical skills count for?** In some disciplines, students spend a considerable proportion of their time developing and practising practical skills. It is important to think clearly about what

contribution to their overall assessment such skills should make, and to let students know this.

8   **May student self-assessment of practical skills be worth using?** Getting students to assess their own practical skills can be one way round the impossible workloads that could be involved if staff were to make all the requisite observations. It is much quicker for staff to moderate student self-assessment of such skills than to undertake the whole task of assessing them.

9   **May student peer assessment of practical skills be worth using?**
Involving students in peer assessment of practical skills can be much less threatening than using tutor assessment. The act of assessing a peer's practical skills is often very good for the peer assessors, in terms of improving their own similar skills, and learning from others' triumphs and disasters.

10 **Is it necessary to have a practical examination?** In some subjects, some sort of end-point practical test may be deemed essential. Driving tests, for example, could not be wholly replaced by a written examination on the Highway Code.

11 **Reserve some marks for the processes.** Help students to see that practical work is not just about reaching a defined end point, but also about the processes and skills involved in doing so successfully.

12 **Ask students to include in their reports 'ways I would do the experiment better next time'.** This encourages students to become more self-aware of how well (or otherwise) they are approaching practical tasks.

13 **Add some 'supplementary questions' to report briefings.** Make these questions that students can answer only when they have thought through their own practical work. For example, students can be briefed to compare their findings with those of a given published source, and comment on any differences in the procedures used in the published work from those they used themselves.

14 **Design the right end products.** Sometimes it is possible to design final outcomes that can be reached only when the practical work itself is of high quality. For example, in chemistry the skills demonstrated in the preparation and refinement of a compound can often be reflected in the purity and amount of the final product.

20

Portfolios

Building up portfolios of evidence of achievement is becoming much more common, following on from the use of Records of Achievement at school. Typically, portfolios are compilations of evidence of students' achievements, including major pieces of their work, feedback comments from tutors, and reflective analyses by the students themselves. It seems probable that, in due course, degree classifications will no longer be regarded as sufficient evidence of students' knowledge, skills and competences, and that profiles will be used increasingly to augment the indicators of students achievements, with portfolios to provide in-depth evidence. Probably the most effective way of leading students to generate portfolios is to build them in as an assessed part of a course. Here the intention is to alert you to some of the more general features to take into account when assessing student portfolios. You may, however, also be thinking about building your own portfolio as evidence concerning your teaching practice, and can build on some of the suggestions given here to make this process more effective and efficient.

Table 11 Advantages and disadvantages of assessment via students' portfolios

Advantages	Disadvantages
• **Validity can be high.** Portfolios can tell much more about students than exam results. They can contain evidence reflecting a wide range of skills and attributes, and can reflect students' work at its best, rather than just a cross-section on a particular occasion. • **Authenticity can be readily tested using even a very short viva or interview.** It only takes a minute or two to question someone on the portfolio they have presented, to check	• **Portfolios take a lot of looking at!** The same difficulty extends beyond assessment; even though portfolios may contain material of considerable interest and value to prospective employers, it is still much easier to draw up interview shortlists on the basis of paper qualifications and grades. • **Portfolios are much harder to mark objectively.** Because of the individual nature of portfolios, it is harder to decide on a set of assessment criteria that will

Table 11 continued

Advantages	Disadvantages
out that it really is their work that we're assessing.	be equally valid across a diverse set of portfolios. This problem can, however, be
• **Portfolios can reflect development.** Most other forms of assessment are more like 'snapshots' of particular levels of development, but portfolios can illustrate progression. This information reflects how fast students can learn from feedback, and is especially relevant to employers of graduates straight from university.	overcome by specifying most of the criteria for assessing portfolios in a relatively generic way, while still leaving room for topic-specific assessment.
• **Portfolios can reflect attitudes and values as well as skills and knowledge.** This too makes them particularly useful to employers looking for the 'right kind' of applicants for jobs. Portfolios can allow students to demonstrate individual strengths, particularly those derived from previous off-campus or on-campus learning experiences or not.	• **The ownership of the evidence can sometimes be in doubt.** It may be necessary to couple the assessment of portfolios with some kind of oral assessment or interview to authenticate or validate the origin of the contents of portfolios, particularly when much of the evidence is genuinely based on the outcomes of collaborative work.

Designing and assessing portfolios

1 **Specify or negotiate intended learning outcomes clearly.** Ensure that students have a shared understanding of the level expected of their work.

2 **Propose a general format for the portfolio**. This helps students demonstrate their achievement of the learning outcomes in ways that are more easily assembled.

3 **Specify or negotiate the nature of the evidence that students should collect.** This makes it easier to assess portfolios fairly, as well as more straightforward for students.

4 **Specify or negotiate the range and extent of the evidence expected from students.** This helps students plan the balance of their work effectively, and helps them avoid spending too much time on one part of their portfolio while missing out important details in other parts.

5 **Don't underestimate the time it takes to assess portfolios.** Also, don't

underestimate their weight and volume if you have a set of them to carry around with you!

6   **Prepare a pro forma to help you assess portfolios.** It is helpful to be able to tick off the achievement of each learning outcome and make decisions about the quality of the evidence as you work through a portfolio.

7   **Use Post-it™ notes to identify parts of the portfolio you may want to return to.** This can save a lot of looking backwards and forwards through a portfolio in search of something you know you've seen in it somewhere!

8   **Consider using Post-its™ to draft your feedback comments.** You can then compose elements of your feedback as you work through the portfolio, instead of having to try to carry it all forward in your mind till you've finished looking at the portfolio.

9   **Put a limit on the physical size of the portfolio.** A single box file is ample for most purposes, or a specified size of ring binder can provide guidance concerning the overall size.

10 **Give guidance on audio or video elements.** Where students are to include video or audio tapes, it is worth limiting the duration of the elements they can include. Insist that they wind the tapes to the point at which they want you to start viewing or listening, otherwise you can spend ages trying to find the bit that they intend you to assess.

11 **Provide interim assessment opportunities.** Give candidates the opportunity to receive advice on whether the evidence they are assembling is appropriate.

12 **Quality, not quantity, counts.** Students should be advised not to submit every piece of paper they have collected over the learning period, otherwise the volume of material can be immense.

13 **Get students to provide route maps.** Portfolios are easier to assess if the material is carefully structured, and accompanied by a reflective account that not only outlines the contents but also asserts which of the criteria each piece of evidence contributes towards.

14 **Get students to provide a structure.** Portfolio elements should be clearly labelled and numbered for easy reference. If loose-leaf folders are used, dividers should be labelled so as to provide easy access to the material. All supplementary material such as audio tapes, videos, drawings, computer programs, tables, graphs, and so on should be appropriately marked and cross-referenced.

15   **Be clear about what you are assessing.** While detailed mark schemes are not really appropriate for portfolios, it is still necessary to have clear and explicit criteria, both for the students' use and to guide assessment.

16   **Structure your feedback.** Students may well have spent many hours assembling portfolios and may have a great deal of personal investment in them. To give their work number marks only (or pass/fail awards) may seem small reward. Consider using an assessment pro forma so that your notes and comments can be directly relayed to the students, particularly in cases where required elements are incomplete or missing.

17   **Encourage creativity.** For some students, this may be the first time they have been given an opportunity to present their strengths in a different way. Hold a brainstorming session about the possible contents of portfolios – for example, which may include videos, recorded interviews, newspaper articles, and so on.

18   **Provide opportunities for self-assessment.** When the students have completed their portfolios, a valuable learning experience in itself is to let the students assess them. A short exercise is to ask them, 'In the light of your experience of producing a portfolio, what do you consider you did especially well, and what would you now do differently?'

19   **Assess in a team.** If possible, set aside a day for you and your colleagues to meet as a team. Write your comments about each portfolio and then pass them round for others to add to. In this way, students get feedback that is more comprehensive, and assessors have the chance to see a more diverse range of portfolios.

20   **Set up an exhibition.** Portfolios take a long time to complete and assess. By displaying them (with students' permission), their valuable experience can be shared.

21   **Think about where and when you will mark portfolios.** They are not nearly as portable as scripts, and you may need equipment such as video or audio playback facilities in order to review evidence. It may be helpful therefore to set aside time when you can book a quiet, well-equipped room where you are able to spread out materials and look at a number of portfolios together. This will help you get an overview, and makes it easier to get a feel for standards.

Case Study: an example of a portfolio assessment pro forma

Figure 2 illustrates how a single sheet can be used to gain an overall impression of the portfolios produced by lecturers on a course leading to a university postgraduate certificate of teaching and learning in higher education. Four almost identical versions of the pro forma can be used as follows:

1   for lecturers to elicit peer feedback from anyone of their choice, so that they can make adjustments before submitting their portfolios;

2   for lecturers' mentors to use to provide feedback to candidates before they submit their portfolios, so that they can make adjustments where necessary before submission;

3   for lecturers themselves to self-assess their portfolio at the point of submission;

4   for the examiners to use to assess the portfolios after submission.

When all four copies of the pro forma are laid out and compared, a quick impression can be gained of the overall quality of the portfolios, and the examiners can decide where to focus their attention – for example, when particular criteria are not fully met, or particular values not fully evidenced.

Portfolio Assessment Form

Candidate's name:
Assessor's name:
Date of assessment:

Evidence of achievement of learning outcomes:	Fully met	Partially met	Not yet met	Comments
1 Designed a teaching programme or element from a course outline or syllabus.				
2 Used a wide and appropriate range of teaching and learning methods effectively and efficiently, to work with large groups, small groups and one-to-one.				
3 Demonstrated the ability to work with appropriate information and communications technologies to support student learning.				
4 Provided support to students on academic and pastoral matters.				
5 Provided evidence of supporting students' development of key skills to equip them for lifelong learning.				
6 Used a wide range of assessment techniques to assess students' work, and to enable students to monitor their own progress.				
7 Used a range of self-, peer and student monitoring and evaluation techniques.				
8 Performed effectively the teaching support and academic administrative tasks involved in teaching.				

Figure 2 Portfolio assessment form

	Fully evidenced	Partially evidenced	Not yet evidenced	Comments
9 Developed personal and professional coping strategies within the constraints of the institutional setting.				
10 Reflected on personal and professional practice and development.				
11 Assessed future development needs and made a plan for continuing professional development.				
Evidence of underpinning values:	**Fully evidenced**	**Partially evidenced**	**Not yet evidenced**	**Comments**
1 Understanding how students learn.				
2 Recognition of individual difference in learning.				
3 Concern for students' development.				
4 Commitment to scholarship.				
5 Team working.				
6 Practising equal opportunities.				
7 Continued reflection on professional practice.				

Overall recommendation:

Clear pass ☐   **Borderline pass** ☐   **Borderline refer** ☐   **Clear refer** ☐

Signature: ....   **Date:** ....

Figure 2 Portfolio assessment form (continued)

21

Presentations

Giving presentations to an audience requires skills substantially different from those needed for writing answers to exam questions. It can be argued that the communications skills involved in giving good presentations are much more relevant to professional competences needed in the world of work. It is particularly useful to develop students' presentations skills if they are likely to go on to research, so that they can give effective presentations at conferences. It is therefore increasingly common to make assessed presentations part of students' overall assessment diet.

Table 12 Advantages and disadvantages of assessment via students' presentation

Advantages	Disadvantages
• **There is no doubt whose performance is being assessed.** When students give individual presentations, the credit they earn can be duly given to them with confidence. • **Students take presentations quite seriously.** The fact that they are preparing for a public performance usually ensures that their research and preparation are addressed well, and therefore they are likely to engage in deep learning about the topic concerned. • **Presentations can also be done as collaborative work.** When it is less important to award to students individual credit for presentations, the benefits of students' working together as teams, preparing and giving presentations, can be realised.	• **With large classes, a round of presentations takes a long time.** This can be countered by splitting the large class into groups of (say) 20 students and facilitating peer assessment of the presentations within each group on the basis of a set of assessment criteria agreed and weighted by the whole class. • **Some students find giving presentations very traumatic!** However, it can be argued that the same is true of most forms of assessment, not least traditional exams. • **The evidence is transient.** Should an appeal be made, unless the presentations have all been recorded there may be limited evidence available with which to reconsider the merit of a particular presentation.

Table 12 continued

Advantages	Disadvantages
• **Where presentations are followed by question-and-answer sessions, students can develop some of the skills they may need in oral examinations or interviews.** Perhaps the most significant advantage of developing these skills in this way is that students can learn a great deal from watching each other's performances. • **Students can learn a great deal from each other.** This includes content knowledge as well as process skills, especially when students are reporting on individual projects.	• **Presentations cannot be anonymous.** It can prove difficult to eliminate subjective bias. • **Presentations can disadvantage some students disproportionately.** For example, students with some kinds of disability may perform poorly in oral presentations, and may find them unacceptably stressful.

Assessing presentations

1 **Be clear about the purposes of student presentations.** For example, the main purpose could be to develop students' skills at giving presentations, or it could be to cause them to do research and reading and improve their subject knowledge. Usually, several such factors are involved together.

2 **Make the criteria for assessment of presentations clear from the outset.** Students will not then be working in a vacuum and will know what is expected of them.

3 **Get students involved in formulating or weighting the assessment criteria.** This can be done either by allowing them to negotiate the criteria themselves or by giving them plenty of opportunities to interrogate criteria you share with them.

4 **Ensure that students understand the weighting of the criteria.** Help them to know whether the most important aspects of their presentations are to do with the *way* they deliver their contributions (voice, clarity of expression, articulation, body language, use of audio-visual aids, and so on) or with the *content* of their presentations (evidence of research, originality of ideas, effectiveness of argument, ability to answer questions, and so on).

5 **Give students some prior practice at assessing presentations.** It is useful, for example, to give students a dry run at applying the assessment criteria they have devised to one or two presentations on video. The

discussion that this produces usually helps to clarify or improve the assessment criteria.

6   **Let the students have a mark-free rehearsal.** This gives students the chance to become more confident and to make some of the more basic mistakes at a point where it doesn't count against them. Constructive feedback is crucial at this point so that students can learn from the experience.

7   **Involve students in the assessment of their presentations.** When given the chance to assess each other's presentations, they take them more seriously and will learn from the experience. Students merely watching each other's presentations tend to get bored and can switch off mentally. If they are evaluating each presentation using an agreed set of criteria, they tend to engage themselves more fully with the process, and in doing so learn more from the content of each presentation.

8   **Ensure that the assessment criteria span presentation processes and the content of the presentations sensibly.** It can be worth reserving some marks for students' abilities to handle questions after their presentations.

9   **Make up grids using the criteria that have been agreed.** Allocate each criterion a weighting and get all the group to fill in the grids for each presentation. The average peer-assessment mark is likely to be at least as good an estimate of the relative worth of each presentation as would be the view of a single tutor doing the assessment.

10 **Be realistic about what can be achieved.** It is not possible to get 12 five-minute presentations into an hour, as presentations always tend to overrun. It is also difficult to get students to concentrate for more than an hour or two on others' presentations. Where classes are large, consider breaking the audience into groups – for example, dividing a class of 100 into four groups, with students presenting concurrently in different rooms, or at different timetabled slots.

11 **Think about the venue.** Students do not always give of their best in large, echoing tiered lecture theatres (nor do we!). A more intimate flat classroom or smaller room can be less threatening, particularly for inexperienced presenters.

12 **Consider assessing using video tapes.** This can allow the presenters themselves the opportunity to review their performances, and can allow you to assess presentations at a time most suitable to you. Viewing a selection of recorded presentations from earlier rounds can be useful for establishing assessment criteria with students. This sort of evidence of teaching and learning is also useful to show external examiners and quality reviewers.

13   **Start small.** Mini-presentations of a few minutes can be almost as valuable as 20-minute presentations for learning the ropes, especially as introductions to the task of standing up and addressing the peer group.

14   **Check what other presentations students may be doing.** Sometimes it can seem to students that everyone is including presentations in their courses. If students find themselves giving three or four within a month or two, it can be very demanding on their time, and repetitious regarding the processes.

Case Study: a group presentations competition – what would you change here?

The context

This is an account of a prize competition (sponsored by a large oil company) in which 13 groups of students gave six-minute presentations to judges recruited from diverse backgrounds, including the university concerned, local commerce and industry, and representatives from the armed forces and the national broadcasting corporation. Students' presentations were also being assessed by members of their course team, and their marks were to count towards their final-year degree profiles.

There were 23 judges divided into 13 judging 'panels' – mostly two people from different backgrounds working as pairs, but with three solo judges as well. Judge panel 8 (for example) started with the presentation given by Group 8, then went on to Group 9 and so on. Three members of the course team were included among the judges.

The student groups ranged in size from five to seven students. They were briefed to use their discretion as to who did what in the presentations.

The format of the presentations was similar in that each was supported by a PowerPoint presentation prepared by the students, accompanied by a handout.

Judges were briefed to make sure that the presentations were no longer than about the six minutes allotted, and then to ask the groups of students a few questions about their presentation, with the total time not to exceed ten minutes.

An assessment sheet was provided to each judge for each of the presentations. This sheet presented five criteria, with space for comments and notes beneath each criterion.

The event was held in a converted old house. Some student groups had a room to themselves for their presentation. In two of the larger rooms, however, two groups of students made their presentations simultaneously at opposite sides of the rooms, resulting in some distractions both to the groups themselves and to the judges.

It was not expected that all the judges would get round all the presentations in the time available, but it was argued that all judges would see about the same number of presentations, and all the presentations would be judged by about the same number of judges.

At the end of the day, judges were asked to place the presentations in rank order – the best one first, and so on – and hand in a single pro forma with this information to the team organising the event. The three top presentations were then awarded cash prizes donated by the sponsoring company. The exercise also counted towards the students' final-year degree marks, with that element of assessment being carried out by members of the course team, who were spread out among the judging panels.

What happened?

The overall event

As was anticipated, presentations tended to overrun. In most cases, in fact, it was the questioning by the judges that actually overran – the students had on the whole perfected the timing of their actual presentations to keep within the six-minute window allowed.

This meant that – as expected – not all of the judges saw all of the presentations. In fact, individual judge panels saw either seven or eight of the 13 presentations.

Some of the student groups divided the presentation just about equally between members of the group, but one or two groups contained the occasional student who did not make any direct contribution to the presentation or to answering judges' questions.

The ranking forms were duly completed and analysed, and the Pro-Vice Chancellor (Teaching and Learning) who had come in time to see one of the presentations, duly presented the awards to the top three student groups.

The day ended with a buffet with wine and beer for all the students and judges, in celebratory mood.

One particular panel's experience of the event

One panel decided to weight each of the five criteria equally, and to use a five-point scale for each criterion using numbers as follows:

4 = excellent

3 = good

2 = adequate

1 = poor

0 = not achieved at all

After each presentation, the two panel members discussed the criteria and the scores awarded. They broadly agreed, but sometimes differed by a point or two in the individual records they kept.

This panel added up scores at the end of the day, with the top presentation (of the seven that the panel saw) being awarded 15 points and the lowest ones scoring 8 or 9 points. The two members of the panel agreed on the rank order of the top three among the presentations they had seen. This panel regarded the 15-point presentation as a clear leader among those seen.

The panel members were surprised to find that none of the presentations the two members had listed in their top three was awarded a prize. Furthermore, all three of the winning presentations were ones that this panel had *not* seen. The panel could therefore not argue with the overall decision, since it was perfectly possible that the three winning presentations had in fact been better than any seen by that panel.

Task: what was wrong, and how should the event be improved next time round?

Please use the table below (or equivalent) to identify any concerns you have about this event, and alongside suggest what could be done to get over the problems you diagnose.

Table 13 Case-study group presentations competition: your criticisms, and suggestions for improvement

Criticisms	Suggestions

Response to the task

Table 14 summarises our thinking on what could be regarded as 'wrong' with the particular event described above, and our suggestions about how a future event could avoid each of the problems we have identified.

Table 14 Case-study group presentations competition: our criticisms, and suggestions for improvement

Criticisms	Suggestions
Essentially, the process led to norm-referenced assessment rather than criterion-referenced assessment.	Brief all assessors to score each of the criteria in the same way, so that scores for each contribution to the presentations could be systematically analysed, allowing any 'hard' or 'soft' judges to be identified.
The criteria themselves were too broad and vague.	Use checklist questions, including wording along the lines 'how well did it . . . ?', 'to what extent did all group members contribute?', and so on. This would allow scoring to be done in the same way for each presentation by each judge, possibly with a number scale such as '4 = extremely well' to '1 = not at all well'.
Students did not really know how their presentations were being judged.	While they knew the broad (vague) criteria, this did not help them to cater for how judges' minds might apply the criteria in practice. If sharper criteria as suggested above were used, with predetermined quality measures attached to each criterion, students could themselves self-assess their presentations during their preparation and rehearsal, and improve them accordingly.
There was no opportunity for rehearsal of judging.	Have a plenary 'induction' round where all judges did a practice run together on a recorded presentation, then compared scores and worked out the average score. This would help judges to emerge with a shared understanding about how each criterion should be interpreted in practice, and also a feel for whether individual judgements were 'hard' or 'soft' compared to the average.
Not all the judges were able to see all the presentations.	Letting them see all the presentations would lengthen the day necessarily, but if some judges end up seeing mainly the best presentations and others seeing the least good ones, the result cannot be held to be objective.

Table 14 continued

Further suggestions, with more detail about how these could be implemented	
Have more of the judges working together at a time.	For example, have either four or five judges at a time for each presentation. This would avoid the students having to do each presentation 13 times for all the judges to see each one.
Have panel sizes equal throughout.	In the case study as described, most panels were made up of two members; other panels were just one member. If (for example) a particular presentation were seen by three single-member 'panels' and voted top by each, the contribution to the final vote would be only half as strong as if the same presentation had been voted top by six judges from two-member panels.
Have different judges working together in each successive panel.	This would allow the judges to learn from each other's approach to the task and improve the reliability of their judgements as the day went on. This would also prevent any particularly confident or assured judge continuing to unduly influence the same other judges on successive occasions.
Randomise the order in which judges see the presentations.	In the case study as described, 'halo' effects (and the reverse) were possible, for example when judges went from an excellent presentation to a poor one. When *all* judges rotate in the same sequence, the effect is compounded.
Build in more time for each panel of judges to discuss each presentation before recording each panel member's assessment.	In the case study as described, whispered conversations on stairways between sessions were all that was possible as attempts to discuss and debrief after each presentation.
Create opportunities for judges to provide useful feedback on each presentation.	Although there was a box for 'feedback comments', few judges had time to use this, and those who did used it in different ways. Provide feedback starters, such as 'the thing I liked best about this presentation was . . .', and 'the thing that worked least well with this presentation was . . .'. Then the overall feedback could be readily analysed and given back to the student groups, and agreement (and indeed disagreement) between different judges would be visible and quantifiable.

22

Assessing performances

In many universities there are courses in subjects such as creative writing, dance, music, drama, and so on where an element of performance is an integral part of the process. These elements are often regarded as more challenging to assess than, for example, written exams. The advantages and disadvantages shown in Table 15 set the context.

Table 15 Advantages and disadvantages of assessment via student performances

Advantages	Disadvantages
• **Validity is achieved.** What is measured is not just an echo of the evidence of achievement of the intended learning outcomes. For performing arts students, for example, performing is the most important focus for the skills they are developing.	• **Consistency is hard to achieve.** Different performances may have strengths and weaknesses in quite different areas, and it is difficult to formulate a set of assessment criteria that will cater for a range of ways of giving a performance.
• **Authenticity is assured.** There is no doubt whose performance is being measured. Furthermore, the context of the assessed performances can be fine-tuned to be as close as possible to the real-life circumstances for which students may be preparing.	• **Some aspects are transient.** It can be hard to revisit a particular performance, for example to check whether it has been assessed fairly. This problem can be overcome by recording performances, but revisiting particular elements then becomes very time-consuming.
• **Candidates who are not good at written exams gain the opportunity to demonstrate what they can really achieve.** This can help address issues relating to a range of other special educational needs or disabilities.	• **Subjectivity may be present.** In many kinds of performance, judges will hold different views about what makes an excellent performance and an ordinary one.
	• **Equity can be compromised.** In group performances, it is hard to arrange for all students to have equal parts to play.

Preparing to assess performances

1   **Clear criteria for assessed performances are absolutely vital.** In the aesthetic domain it is sometimes difficult to articulate these criteria without reducing them to absurdia. The key is to produce criteria that assess the essence of the performance rather than the easy-to-measure elements.

2   **Learn from the experience of others.** To develop expertise in assessing performances, it is invaluable to work alongside more experienced colleagues and learn from the ways in which they make evaluations or judgements.

3   **Ensure that the evidence concerning the elements of the performances is recorded.** Use video, audio tape, notation or other methods, so there is evidence subsequently available for moderation.

4   **Stage assessment over a period of time.** It is often helpful to have an incremental element to the assessment so that 'work in progress' assessed at intermediate points contributes to the final grade.

5   **Require students to keep careful records of their preparations for the performances.** This makes it possible for their reflections on the processes, by which their performances were developed, to contribute to their assessment.

6   **Include peer assessment.** Other students on a course can contribute to the assessment of each other's performances, so long as the assessment criteria are explicit and the evidence of successful outcomes is required. Intra-group peer assessment can also be helpful – for example, with students who are performing together in a play or dance performance.

7   **Include self-assessment.** While it may not be possible to self-assess performances in a detached, objective manner, getting students to self-assess their performance can lead them into useful reflection, and deepen the learning they gain from their own performances. The self-assessment can open up valuable dialogue with tutors and fellow learners.

8   **Minimise unhelpful kinds of competition.** Students in the performing arts move in a competitive world, but assessment schemes that prioritise 'the best' and 'winning' can be counter-productive in contexts where peer support and peer assessment are interdependent.

9   **Use audiences to contribute to the assessment.** Performances often provide excellent opportunities for gaining a range of views of achievement. Beware, however, of candidates packing audiences with their fans and friends, and devise criteria that are quantifiable as well as qualitative.

10 **Be aware of the stresses that performances can put on candidates.** In addition to the performance anxiety that is common in most kinds of assessment, there are further stresses that can occur. Examples include falling scenery (or falling people), damaged instruments, failing audio-visual equipment, and injuries befalling performers. Aim to develop styles of assessment that can accommodate glitches, and ensure that such happenings don't necessarily indicate complete failure.

23

Student projects

In many courses, one of the most important kinds of work undertaken by students takes the form of individual projects, often relating theory to practice beyond the college environment. Such projects are usually an important element in the overall work of each student, and are individual in nature.

Table 16 Advantages and disadvantages of assessment via project work

Advantages	Disadvantages
• **Project work gives students the opportunity to develop their strategies for tackling research questions and scenarios.** Students' project work often counts significantly in their final-year degree performance, and research opportunities for the most successful students may depend primarily on the skills they demonstrated through project work. • **Projects can be integrative.** They can help students to link theories to practice and to bring together different topics (and even different disciplines) into a combined frame of reference. • **Project work can help assessors to identify the best students.** Because project work necessarily involves a significant degree of student autonomy, it does not favour those students who just happen to be good at tackling traditional assessment formats.	• **Project work takes a lot of marking!** Each project is different and needs to be assessed carefully. It is not possible for assessors to 'learn the scheme and steam ahead' when marking a pile of student projects. • **Projects are necessarily different.** This means that some will be 'easier', some will be tough, and it becomes difficult to decide how to balance the assessment dividend between students who tackled something straightforward and did it well, as opposed to students who tried something really difficult and got bogged down in it. • **Projects are relatively final.** They are usually one-off elements of assessment. When students fail to complete a project, or fail to get a difficult one started at all, it is rarely feasible to set them a replacement one.

Designing student projects

Setting, supporting and assessing such work can be a significant part of the work of a lecturer, and the following suggestions should help to make these tasks more manageable.

1   **Choose the learning by doing to be relevant and worthwhile.** Student projects are often the most significant and extended parts of their courses, and it is important that the considerable amount of time they may spend on them is useful to them and relevant to the overall learning outcomes of the courses or modules with which the projects are associated.

2   **Work out specific learning outcomes for the projects.** These will be of an individual nature for each project, as well as including general ones relating to the course area in which the project is located.

3   **Formulate projects so that they address higher-level skills appropriately.** The aims of project work are often to bring together threads from different course areas or disciplines, and to allow students to demonstrate the integration of their learning.

4   **Give students as much opportunity as possible to select their own projects.** When students have a strong sense of ownership of the topics of their projects, they put much more effort into their work, and are more likely to be successful.

5   **Include scope for negotiation and adjustment of learning outcomes.** Project work is necessarily more like research than other parts of students' learning. Students need to be able to adjust the range of a project to follow through interesting or important aspects that they discover along the way. Remember that it is still important to set standards, and the scope for negotiation may sometimes be restricted to ways that students will go about accumulating evidence to match set criteria.

6   **Make the project briefings clear, and ensure that they will provide a solid foundation for later assessment.** Criteria should be clear, and well understood by students at the start of their work on projects.

7   **Keep the scope of project work realistic.** Remember that students will usually have other kinds of work competing for their time and attention, and it is tragic when students succeed with project work, only to fail other parts of their courses to which they should have devoted more time alongside their projects. Students sometimes become inappropriately obsessive concerning a project.

8   **Liaise with library and information services colleagues.** When a number of projects make demands on the availability of particular learning resources or information technology facilities, it is important to arrange this in advance with such colleagues, so that they can be ready to ensure that students are able to gain access to the resources they will need.

9   **Ensure that a sensible range of factors will be assessed.** Assessment needs to relate to work that encompasses the whole of the project, and shall not be unduly skewed towards such skills as writing up or oral presentation. These are likely to be assessed in any case in other parts of students' work.

10   **Collect a library of past projects.** This can be of great help to students starting out on their own projects, and can give them a realistic idea of the scope of the work likely to be involved, as well as ideas on ways to present their work well.

11   **Arrange staged deadlines for projects.** It is very useful for students to be able to receive feedback on plans for their project work so that they can be steered away from going off at tangents, or from spending too much time on particular aspects of a project.

12   **Allow sufficient time for project work.** The outcomes of project work may well include students' developing time-management and task-management skills along the way, but they need time and support to do this. Arrange contact windows so that students with problems are not left too long without help.

13   **Consider making projects portfolio based.** Portfolios often represent the most flexible and realistic way of assessing project work, and allow appendices containing a variety of evidence to be presented along with the more important parts showing students' analysis, thinking, argument and conclusions.

14   **Encourage students to give each other feedback on their project work.** This can be extended to elements of peer assessment, but it is more important simply to get students talking to each other about their work in progress. Such feedback can help students sort out many of the problems they encounter during project work, and can improve the overall standard of their work.

15   **Think about the spaces and places that students will use to do their project work.** Some of the work may well occur off-campus, but it remains important that students have access to suitable places to write up and prepare their project work for assessment, as well as facilities and support to help them analyse the data and materials they accumulate.

16   **Include a self-evaluation component in each project.** This allows students to reflect on their project work and think more deeply about what went well and where there may have been problems. It can be particularly useful to students to get feedback about the quality of their self-evaluation.

24

Poster displays and exhibitions

When students are asked to synthesise the outcomes of their learning and/ or research into a self-explanatory poster (individually or in groups) that can be assessed on the spot, it can be an extremely valuable process. More and more conferences are providing poster-display opportunities as an effective way of disseminating findings and ideas. This kind of assessment can provide practice in developing the skills relevant to communicating by such visual means.

Table 17 Advantages and disadvantages of assessment via poster displays and exhibitions

Advantages	Disadvantages
• **Poster displays and exhibitions can be a positive step towards diversifying assessment.** Some students are much more at home producing something visual, or something tangible, than at meeting the requirements of traditional assessment formats such as exams, essays or reports.	• **Subjectivity may creep in.** However valid the assessment may be, it can be more difficult to make the assessment of posters or exhibitions demonstrably reliable. It is harder to formulate 'hard' assessment criteria for diverse assessment artefacts, and a degree of subjectivity may necessarily creep into their assessment.
• **Poster displays and exhibitions can provide opportunities for students to engage in peer assessment.** The act of participating in the assessment process deepens students' learning and can add variety to their educational experience.	• **It may be harder to bring the normal quality assurance procedures into assessment of this kind, if the outputs are ephemeral.** For example, it can be difficult to bring in external examiners, or to preserve the artefacts upon which assessment decisions have been made so that assessment can be revisited if necessary (for example, for candidates who end up on degree classification borderlines).
• **Such assessment formats can help students to develop a wide range of useful, transferable skills.** This can pave the way towards the effective communication of research findings, as well as developing communication skills	• **It can take more effort to link assessment of this sort to stated**

Table 17 continued

Advantages	Disadvantages
in directions complementary to those involving the written (or printed) word. • **Poster displays or exhibitions can enable staff to assess fast in real time.** This can make for variety and be a refreshing change compared to assessing written assignments.	**intended learning outcomes.** This is not least because poster displays and exhibitions are likely to be addressing a range of learning outcomes simultaneously, some of which are subject based, but others of which will address the development of key transferable skills.

Planning assessed poster displays and exhibitions

1   **Use the assessment process as a showcase.** Students are often rather proud of their achievements, and it can be invaluable to invite others in to see what has been achieved. Think about inviting moderators, senior staff, students on parallel courses, and employers. Gather their impressions, either by using a short questionnaire or by orally asking them a couple of relevant questions about their experiences of seeing the display.

2   **Use posters as a way to help other students to learn.** For example, final-year students can produce posters showing the learning they gained during placements. This can be a useful opportunity for students preparing to find their own placements to adjust their approaches and base them on others' experiences.

3   **Get students to peer-assess each other's posters.** Having undertaken the task of making posters themselves, they will be well prepared to review critically the work of others. This also provides chances for them to learn from the research undertaken by the whole cohort rather than just from their own work.

4   **Consider asking students to produce a one-page handout to supplement their poster.** This will test a further set of skills, and will provide all reviewers with an *aide-mémoire* for subsequent use.

5   **Give sufficient time for the debriefing.** Lots of learning takes place in the discussion during and after the display. The tendency is to put poster-display and exhibition sessions on during the last week of the term or semester, and this can give little time to unpack the ideas at the end.

6   **Make careful practical arrangements.** Large numbers of posters take up a lot of display space, and to get the best effect they should be displayed on

boards. Organising this is possible in most universities – for example, by borrowing publicity display boards – but it needs to be planned in advance. Allow sufficient time for students to mount their displays, and make available drawing pins, Blu-Tack™, tape, Velcro™ sticky pads, demountable display equipment, and so on.

7   **Stagger the assessment.** In cases when peers are assessing each other's posters, to avoid collusion, 'fixing' and outbursts of spite it is valuable to arrange that half the display is in one room and the rest in another, or to run successive displays at different times. Number the posters and get half the group to assess the odd-numbered posters and the other half to assess the even-numbered ones, and average the data that are produced.

8   **Consider getting groups to produce a poster between them.** This encourages collaborative working and can reduce the overall numbers of posters – useful when student numbers are large. You could then consider getting students within the group to peer-assess (intra) their respective contributions to the group as well as to assess collaboratively the posters of the other groups (inter-peer group assessment).

9   **Link assessment of poster displays to open days.** From looking at posters on display, students coming to visit the institution when they are considering applying for courses may well get a good idea of what students actually do on the courses.

10 **Prepare a suitable assessment sheet.** Base this firmly on the assessment criteria for the exercise. Provide space for peers' comments. This paves the way towards plenty of opportunity for peer feedback.

11 **Use assistance.** When working with large numbers of peer-assessed posters, you may need help in working out the averaged scores. Either get the students to do the number work for themselves or for each other (and advise them that the numbers will be randomly checked to ensure fair play). Alternatively, press-gang colleagues, partners, administrators or progeny to help with the task.

12 **Provide a rehearsal opportunity.** Let the students have a practice run at a relatively early stage, using a mock-up or a draft on flip-chart paper. Give them feedback on these drafts, and let them compare their ideas. This can help them to avoid the most obvious disasters later.

13 **Let everyone know why they are using poster displays.** This method of assessment may be unfamiliar to students and to your colleagues. It is therefore valuable if you can provide a clear justification to all concerned of the educational merits of the method.

14 **Brief students really carefully about what is needed.** Ideally, let them see a whole range of posters from previous years (or some mock-ups, or photographs of previous displays) so that they have a good idea about the requirements without having their originality and creativity suppressed.

15 **Use the briefing to discuss criteria and weighting.** Students will need to know what level of effort they should put into different elements such as presentation, information content, structure, visual features, and so on. If students are not clear about this, you may well end up with brilliantly presented posters with little relevance to the topic, or really dull, dense posters that try to compress the text of a long report onto a single A1 sheet.

16 **Give students some practical guidelines.** Let them know how many A1 sheets they can have, where their work will be displayed, what print size the text should be in order to be readable on a poster, what resources will be available to them in college, and how much help they can get from outsiders such as friends on other courses who take good photographs or who have the knack of writing in attractive script.

17 **Attach a budget to the task.** In poster displays, money shows! If you were to give a totally free hand to students, the ones with the best access to photocopiers, photographic resources, expensive papers, word processors, and so on might well produce better-looking products than students who have little money to spend on their posters or displays (although it does not always turn out this way). Giving a notional budget can help to level the playing field, as can requiring students to use only items from a given list, with materials perhaps being limited to those provided in workshops in the college.

18 **Keep records of poster displays and exhibitions.** Take photographs or make a short video. It is not always possible to retain complete displays and exhibitions, but a handy reminder can be very useful when planning the next similar event. Evidence of the displays can also be interesting to external examiners and quality reviewers.

19 **Get someone (or a group) to provide a 'guide booklet' to the exhibition.** This helps the students undertaking this task to make relative appraisals of the different items or collections making up the exhibition as a whole.

20 **Consider turning it into a celebration as well.** After the assessment has taken place, it can be pleasurable to provide some refreshments, and make the display or exhibition part of an end-of-term or end-of-course celebration.

25

Dissertations and theses

Students invest a great deal of time and energy in producing dissertations and theses, usually in their final year. Sometimes these arise from the results of their project work. We therefore owe it to them to mark them fairly and appropriately. Moreover, these forms of assessment extend to postgraduate work, where the validity, reliability and transparency of our assessment become even more critical, as then dissertations or theses are usually the most important assessed elements of students' achievement.

Table 18 Advantages and disadvantages of assessment via dissertations and theses

Advantages	Disadvantages
• **Dissertations and theses are individual in nature.** There are reduced possibilities regarding plagiarism and cheating, and a greater confidence that we are assessing the work of individual students. • **There is usually double or multiple marking.** Because dissertations and theses are important assessment artefacts, more care is taken to ensure that the assessment is as objective as possible. • **There is usually further triangulation.** External examiners are often asked to oversee the assessment of at least a cross-section of dissertations or theses, and sometimes see all of them. The fact that such triangulation exists is a further pressure towards making the assessment reliable and valid in the first instance.	• **Assessment takes a long time.** Even more so than with student projects, dissertations or theses are so individual that it is not possible for assessors to 'get into their stride' and forge ahead marking large numbers of these in a given period of time. • **Assessment can involve subjectivity.** For example, it is less possible to achieve 'anonymous' marking with large-scale artefacts such as these, as the first assessor at least is likely to have been supervising or advising the candidate along the route towards assessment. • **Assessment can be over-dominated by matters of style and structure.** While both of these are important and deserve to contribute towards the assessment of dissertations or theses, there is abundant evidence that a well-structured, fluent piece of work

Table 18 continued

Advantages	Disadvantages
	whose actual content is quite modest attracts higher ratings than a less well structured, somewhat 'jerky' piece of work whose content is of a higher quality.

Assessing dissertations and theses

1   **Make sure that the assessment criteria are explicit, clear, and understood by the students.** This may seem obvious! However, theses and dissertations are normally very different in the topics and themes they address, and the assessment criteria need to accommodate such differences. Students will naturally compare marks and feedback comments. The availability of clear criteria helps them see that their work has been assessed fairly.

2   **Get students to assess a few past dissertations.** You can't expect them to do this at the same level as may be appropriate for 'real' assessment, but you can (for example) issue students with a one-sided pro forma questionnaire to complete as they study examples of dissertations. Include questions about the power of the introduction, the quality and consistency of referencing, and the coherence of the conclusions.

3   **Offer guidance and support to students throughout the process.** Dissertations usually take students quite some time to complete. Students appreciate, and need, some help along the route. It is worth holding tutorials both individually and with groups. This takes good planning, and dates need to be set well in advance and published on a notice board or in a handout to students.

4   **Ensure that student support mechanisms are available.** With large class sizes, we cannot afford to spend many hours of staff time with individual students. However, students can draw much valuable support from other students if we facilitate ways of their helping each other. Consider introducing supplemental instruction processes, or setting up friendly yet critical student syndicates. Running a half-day workshop with students counselling each other can be valuable.

5   **Beware of the possibility of bias.** Sometimes dissertations involve students writing on topics of a culturally or politically sensitive nature. We need to be aware of any prejudices of our own, and to compensate for any bias these

could cause in our assessment. Whenever possible, dissertations should be second-marked (at least!).

6   **Can you provide students with equal opportunities regarding selecting their dissertation themes?** Research for some dissertations will involve students in visiting outside agencies, finding materials for experiments, building models, and so on. With resource limitations becoming more severe, students may be forced to avoid certain topics altogether. Try to suggest to students topics for which the financial implications are manageable.

7   **Check whether dissertations always have to be bound.** This may depend on which year of the course they are set in. It may be worth reserving binding for final-year dissertations, to help save students money and to make updating possible if required.

8   **Help students to monitor their own progress.** It helps to map the assessment criteria in a way that helps students to keep track of their own progress and achievements. Computer programs are now available that help students work out how they are getting on, and prompt them to the next steps they should be considering at each stage.

9   **When assessing dissertations, collect a list of questions to select from at a forthcoming viva.** Even if there is not going to be a viva, such lists of questions can be a useful addition to the feedback you return to students.

10 **Use Post-it™ notes while assessing dissertations and theses.** These can be placed towards the edges of pages, so that notes and questions written on the Post-its™ can be found easily again. They help you avoid having to write directly on the pages of the dissertation or thesis (especially when your questions are found to be addressed two pages later!).

26

Work-based learning

Increasing use is being made of assessment based on students' performance in the workplace, whether on placements, as part of work-based learning programmes or during practice elements of courses. Often, a variety of assessors are used, sometimes giving rise to concerns about how consistent assessment practice between the workplace and the institution can be assured. Traditional means of assessment are often unsuitable in contexts where what is important is not easily measured by written accounts. Many courses include a placement period, and the increasing use of accreditation of prior experiential learning in credit accumulation systems means that we need to look at ways of assessing material produced by students in work contexts, rather than just things students write up when back at college after their placements.

Table 19 Advantages and disadvantages of assessment via work-based learning

Advantages	Disadvantages
• **Work-based learning can balance the assessment picture.** Future employers are likely to be at least as interested in students' work-related competences as in their academic performance, and assessing work-based learning can give useful information about students' competences beyond the curriculum. • **Assessing placement learning helps students to take placements more seriously.** As with anything else, if they're not assessed, some students will not really get down to learning from their placements. • **Assessing placement learning helps to make your other assessments closer to practice.** Although it is difficult to assess placement learning	• **Reliability of assessment is difficult to achieve.** Placements tend to be highly individual, and students' opportunities to provide evidence that lends itself well to assessment can vary greatly from one placement to another. • **Some students will have much better placements than others.** Some students will have the opportunity to demonstrate their flair and potential, while others will be constrained into relatively routine work practices. • **There may be financial implications.** Work-based assessors may be reluctant to undertake the task without payment. • **Constructive alignment may be difficult to achieve.** It may be problematic to fully align work-based

Table 19 continued

Advantages	Disadvantages
reliably, the validity of the related learning may outweigh this difficulty and help you to tune in more successfully to real-world problems, situations and practices in the rest of your assessment practice. • **Assessing placement learning can bring you closer to employers who can help you.** It is sometimes possible to involve external people such as employers in some in-college forms of assessment, for example student presentations, interview technique practising, and so on. The contacts you make with employers during placement supervision and assessment can help you to identify those who have much to offer you.	learning opportunities with the intended learning outcomes of the course or module, because of the individual nature of work-based learning. • **It can be disaster-prone.** Sometimes work-based learning goes wrong, or throws up uncontrollable contingencies or disasters, which can have a significant impact on the performance of the students affected.

Assessing work-based learning

The following suggestions may help you to strike an appropriate balance between validity and reliability if your assessment agenda includes assessing work-based learning, whether associated with work placements or arising from a need to accredit prior experiential learning.

1 **Explore how best you can involve employers, professional supervisors and colleagues.** They will need careful briefing, and negotiation may also be required to achieve their full co-operation, as they (like you!) are often very busy people. Ways of involving them include asking them to produce testimonials, statements of competence, checklists, grids and pro formas, or simply to sign off students' own statements of competence or achievement.

2 **Be clear about the purpose of the assessment.** Is the assessment being done to satisfy a funding body, or because it is required by the university, or because the employers wish it to be done? Or is the assessment primarily to aid students' learning? Or is it primarily designed to help students develop skills and experience that will aid their future careers? Clarifying the purposes can help you decide the most appropriate forms of assessment.

3 **Get the balance right.** Work out carefully what proportion of students' overall assessment will be derived from their placements. Decide whether

the related assessment should be on a pass–fail basis or whether an attempt should be made to classify the students' placement work for degrees.

4   **Expect placements to be very different.** If a group of students are spread through a number of companies or organisations, some will have a very good experience of placement, whereas others, through no fault of their own, can have an unsatisfactory experience. It is important that factors outside students' control are not allowed to prejudice assessment.

5   **Consider carefully whether a mentor is well placed to assess.** There can sometimes be complex confusions of role if the person who is the professional supporter or friend of the student whose performance is being assessed is also the person who has to make critical evaluations for assessment purposes.

6   **Decide carefully whether to tutor-assess during workplace visits.** Visiting students on placement certainly gives tutors opportunities to gather data that may be relevant to assessment, but if assessment is on the agenda, the whole nature of such visits changes. One way of separating the assessment ethos from the workplace environment is to handle at least some face-to-face meetings with students off-site rather than at the workplace.

7   **Consider including the assessment of a work log.** Some professions prescribe the exact form that such a log or work diary should take; in other work contexts it is possible for the course team or the students themselves to devise their own formats. It is often helpful if such logs include lists of learning outcomes, skills or competences that students are expected to achieve and demonstrate, with opportunities to check these off and add comments as appropriate. It can be even better to encourage students to express as learning outcomes *unanticipated* learning that they discover happening to them during a placement. Some of these outcomes may be more important than the intended ones.

8   **Ask students to produce a reflective journal.** This can be a much more personal kind of document, and might include hopes, fears and feelings as well as more mundane accounts of actions and achievements. Assessing reflective journals can raise tricky issues of confidentiality and disclosure, but ways round such issues can be found, particularly if students are asked to submit for assessment edited extracts from their reflective journals.

9   **Consider using a portfolio.** A portfolio to demonstrate achievement at work can include suitably anonymised real products from the workplace (with the permission of the employer) as well as testimonials from clients, patients, support staff and others.

10   **Help to ensure that assessment does not blind students to their learning on placement.** Consider asking students who have completed work placements to write their experiences up in the form of a journal article, perhaps for an in-house magazine or journal. A collection of these writings can help to disseminate their experiences. Joint articles written with employers are even more valuable, and help make links with employers better.

Chapter 4

Feedback and assessment

27 Quality of feedback
28 Helping students to make the most of your feedback
29 Reducing your load: short cuts to good feedback
30 Feedback in writing or print
31 Face-to-face feedback
32 Electronic feedback

27

Quality of feedback

If 'assessment is the engine that drives learning' (John Cowan), then the ways in which we give feedback are important in gearing and lubricating the engine so that maximum effect is achieved from the effort put in by all concerned. How can we best give feedback to students? This chapter explores a variety of ways in which feedback can be given to students and includes many suggestions for optimising the usefulness of such feedback. We can select from a wide range of processes, but we also need to address as many as possible of a range of qualities and attributes in our strategy for providing feedback.

For example, feedback needs to be:

- **Timely – the sooner the better.** There has been plenty of research into how long after the learning event it takes for the effects of feedback to be significantly eroded. Ideally, feedback should be received within a day or two, and is even better if given almost straight away, as is possible (for example) in some computer-aided learning situations, and equally in some face-to-face contexts. When marked work is returned to students weeks (or even months) after submission, feedback is often totally ignored because it bears little relevance to students' current needs then. Many institutions nowadays specify in their student charters that work should be returned within two to three weeks, enabling students to derive greater benefits from feedback. When feedback is received very quickly, it is much more effective, as students can still remember exactly what they were thinking as they addressed each task.

- **Personal and individual.** Feedback needs to fit each student's achievement, individual nature and personality. Global ways of compiling and distributing feedback can reduce the extent of ownership that students feel over the feedback they receive, even when the quality and amount of feedback are increased. Each student is still a person.

- **Articulate.** Students should not have to struggle to make sense of our feedback. Whether our messages are congratulatory or critical, it should be easy for students to work out exactly what we are trying to tell them. They should not have to read each sentence more than once, trying to work out what we are really saying.

- **Empowering.** If feedback is intended to strengthen and consolidate learning, we need to make sure it doesn't dampen learning down. This is easier to ensure when feedback is positive, of course, but we need to look carefully at how best we can make critical feedback equally empowering to learners. We must not forget that often feedback is given and received in a system in which power is loaded towards the provider of the feedback rather than the recipient – for example, where we are driving assessment systems.

- **Manageable.** There are two sides to this. From our point of view, designing and delivering feedback to students could easily consume all the time and energy we have – it is an endless task. But also from students' point of view, getting too much feedback can result in their not being able to sort out the important feedback from the routine feedback, reducing their opportunity to benefit from the feedback they need most.

- **Developmental.** Feedback should open doors, not close them. In this respect, we have to be particularly careful with the words we use when giving feedback to students. Clearly, words with such 'final language' implications as 'weak' or 'poor' cause irretrievable breakdowns in the communication between assessor and student. To a lesser extent, even positive words such as 'excellent' can cause problems when feedback on the next piece of work is only 'very good' – why wasn't it excellent again? In all such cases it is better to praise exactly what *was* very good or excellent in a little more detail, rather than take the short cut of just using the adjectives themselves.

28

Helping students to make the most of your feedback

The suggestions below unpack how you can set about trying to ensure that the feedback you provide for your students addresses the factors listed in the previous section. Furthermore, some of the suggestions that follow are intended to help you to maintain high-quality feedback to your students without consuming inordinate amounts of your precious time and energy.

1 **Try to do more than put ticks.** Tempting as it is to put ticks beside things that are correct or good, ticks don't give much real feedback. It takes a little longer to add short phrases such as 'good point', 'I agree with this', 'yes, this is it', 'spot on', and so on, but such feedback comments do much more to motivate students than just ticks. Think about how students will feel when they get marked work back. They can be in states of heightened emotion at such points. If they find their scripts covered with comments in red ink (even when it is all praise), it is rather intimidating for them at first.

2 **Avoid putting crosses if possible.** Students often have negative feelings about crosses on their work, feelings carried forward from schooldays. Short phrases such as 'no', 'not quite', 'but this wouldn't work', and so on can be much better ways of alerting students to things that are wrong.

3 **Try to make your writing legible.** If there is not going to be room to make a detailed comment directly on the script, put code numbers or asterisks and write your feedback on a separate sheet. A useful compromise is to put feedback comments on Post-it™ notes stuck to appropriate parts of a script, but it's worth still using a code, asterisk or some such device so that even if students remove the Post-its™ as they read through their work, they can still work out exactly which points your comments apply to.

4 **Try giving some feedback before you start assessing.** For example, when a class hands in a piece of work, you can at once issue handouts of model answers and discussions of the main things that may have caused

problems. Students can read such information while their own efforts are still fresh in their minds, and can derive a great deal of feedback straight away. You can then concentrate, while assessing, on giving them *additional* feedback individually, without going into detail on things that you have already addressed in the general discussion comments you have already given them.

5   **Give feedback to groups of students sometimes.** This helps students become aware that they are not alone in making mistakes, and allows them to learn from the successes and failures of others.

6   **Let students respond.** When giving one-to-one feedback, it is often useful to allow students the opportunity to interrogate you and challenge your comments (orally or in writing) so that any issues that are unclear can be resolved.

7   **Feedback should be realistic.** When making suggestions for improvement of student work, consider carefully whether they can be achieved. It may not have been possible (for example) for students to gain access to certain resources or books in the time available.

8   **Feedback should be de-linked from wealth!** Check that you are not giving feedback on the amount of money that was spent on the work you mark – for example, when some students can submit work produced using expensive desktop publishing systems, while other students have no access to such facilities.

9   **Feedback should be honest.** When there are serious problems that students need to be made aware of, feedback comments should not skirt round these or avoid them. It may be best to arrange for individual face-to-face feedback sessions with some students, so you can give any bad news in ways that enable you to monitor how they are taking it, and provide appropriate comfort at the same time.

10 **Feedback can be given before scores or grades.** Consider whether sometimes it may be worth returning students' work to them with feedback comments but no grades (but having written down your marks in your own records). Then invite students to try to work out what their scores or grade should be, and to report to you in a week's time what they think. This causes students to read all your feedback comments earnestly in their bid to work out how they have done. Most students will make good guesses regarding their grades, and it's worth finding out which students are way out too.

11 **Think about audio tapes for giving feedback.** In some subjects it is quite hard to write explanatory comments on students' work. For example, in

mathematical problems it can be quicker and easier to 'talk' individual students through how a problem should be solved, referring to asterisks or code numbers marked on their work. Such feedback has the advantages of tone of voice for emphasis and explanation. Another advantage is that students can play the tape repeatedly, until they have fully understood all your feedback.

12   **Consider giving feedback by email.** Some students feel most relaxed when working at a computer terminal on their own. With email, students can receive your feedback when they are ready to think about it. They can read it again later, and even file it. Using email, you can give students feedback asynchronously as you work through their scripts, rather than their having to wait till you return the whole set to a class.

29

Reducing your load: short cuts to good feedback

Keep records carefully . . .

Keeping good records of assessment and feedback takes time, but can save time in the long run. The following suggestions may help you organise your record-keeping.

1   **Be meticulous.** However tired you are at the end of a marking session, record all the marks immediately (or indeed continuously as you go along). Then put the marks in a different place from the scripts. Then, should any disaster befall you (briefcase stolen, house burned down, and so on), there is the chance that you will still have the marks even if you don't have the scripts any longer (or vice versa).

2   **Be systematic.** Use class lists, when available, as the basis of your records. Otherwise, make your own class lists as you go along. File all records of assessment in places where you can find them again. It is possible to spend as much time looking for missing mark sheets as it took to do the original assessment!

3   **Use technology to produce assessment records.** Keep marks on a grid on a computer, or use a spreadsheet, and save by date as a new file every time you add to it, so you are always confident that you are working with the most recent version. Keep paper copies of each list as an insurance against disaster! Keep back-up copies of disks or sheets – simply photocopying a handwritten list of marks is a valuable precaution.

4   **Use technology to save you from number-crunching.** The use of computer spreadsheet programs can allow the machine to do all the sub-totalling, averaging and data handling for you. If you are apprehensive about setting up a system yourself, a computer-loving colleague or a member of the information systems support staff will be delighted to start you off.

5 **Use other people.** Some universities employ administrative staff to issue and collect in work for assessment, and to make up assessment lists and input the data into computers. Partners, friends and even young children can help you check your addition of marks, and help you record the data.

Reduce your burden . . .

The following are some straightforward ways to lighten your assessment and feedback load.

6 **Reduce the number of your assignments.** Are all of them strictly necessary, or is it possible to combine some of them and completely delete others?

7 **Use shorter assignments.** Often we ask for 2,000-, 3,000- or 5,000-word assignments or reports when a fraction of the length might be just as acceptable. Some essays or long reports could be replaced by shorter reviews, articles, memorandum reports or summaries. Projects can be assessed by poster displays instead of reports, and exam papers can include some sections of multiple-choice questions, particularly where these could be marked by optical mark scanners, or by using computer-managed assessment directly.

8 **Use assignment return sheets.** These can be pro formas that contain the assessment criteria for an assignment, with spaces for ticks/crosses, grades, marks and brief comments. They enable rapid feedback to be given on 'routine' assessment matters, providing more time for making individual comments to students when necessary on deeper aspects of their work.

9 **Consider using statement banks.** These are a means whereby your frequently repeated comments can be written once each, then printed or emailed to students, or put onto transparencies or slides for discussion in a subsequent lecture.

10 **Involve students in self-assessment or peer assessment.** Start small, and explain what you are doing and why. Involving students in part of their assessment can provide them with very positive learning experiences.

11 **Mark some exercises in class time using self-marking or peer marking.** This is sometimes useful when students, expecting tutor assessment, have prepared work to the standard that they wish to be seen by you.

12 **Don't count all assessments.** For example, give students the option that their best five out of eight assignments will count as their coursework mark.

Students satisfied with their *first* five need not undertake the other three at all then.

When you still find yourself overloaded . . .

No one wants to have to cope with huge piles of coursework scripts or exam papers. However, not all factors may be within your control, and you may still end up overloaded. The following wrinkles may be somewhat soothing at such times!

13 **Put the great unmarked pile *under* your desk.** It is very discouraging to be continually reminded of the magnitude of the overall task. Keep only a handful of scripts or assignments in sight – about as many as you might expect to deal with in about an hour.

14 **Set yourself progressive targets.** Plan to accomplish a bit more at each stage than you need to. Build in safety margins. This allows you some insurance against unforeseen disasters (and children), and can allow you gradually to earn some time off as a bonus.

15 **Make an even better marking scheme.** Often, it only becomes possible to make a really good marking scheme after you've found out the ways in which candidates are actually answering the questions. Put the marking scheme where you can see it easily. It can be useful to paste it up with Blu-Tack above your desk or table, so you don't have to rummage through your papers looking for it every time you need it.

16 **Mark in different places!** Mark at work, at home, and anywhere else that's not public. This means, of course, carrying scripts around, as well as your marking scheme (or a copy of it). It does, however, avoid one place becoming so associated with doom and depression that you develop place-avoidance strategies for it!

17 **First mark one question through all the scripts.** This allows you to become quickly skilled at marking that question, without the agenda of all the rest of the questions on your mind. It also helps ensure reliability and objectivity of marking. When you've completely mastered your marking scheme for all questions, start marking whole scripts.

18 **If you really can't cope, ask for help.** You can get away with this once or twice in your assessing career, but if you do it too often you will make yourself unpopular.

30

Feedback in writing or print

This section is about hard-copy feedback, whether written directly onto students' assessed work or supplied in writing or print alongside returned work. (We will consider electronic feedback later.) A clear advantage of hard-copy feedback is that it is enduring, and can be viewed and reviewed again by students (and indeed by assessors themselves and quality reviewers). In the pages that follow, we'll explore half a dozen of the range of processes involving feedback in writing or print. You'll be able to think of other ways of combining these, and alternatives that may have more advantages and fewer drawbacks.

Handwritten comments

Handwritten comments on (or about) students' assessed work are one of the most widely used forms of feedback to students. They include our written feedback on essays, reports, dissertations, solutions to problems, and so on. Not so long ago, there were few alternatives to this way of giving students feedback on their work, and the written comments were usually accompanied by an assessment judgement of one kind or another.

Table 20 Advantages and disadvantages of feedback presented via handwritten comments

Advantages	Disadvantages
• Feedback can be personal, individual, and directly related to the particular piece of work. • Feedback may be regarded as authoritative and credible. • The feedback can be tailored to justify an accompanying assessment judgement.	• Handwritten feedback can be hard to read! • When it is critical, handwritten feedback – because of its authoritativeness – can be threatening. • It is slow and time-consuming to write individually on (or about)

Table 20 continued

Advantages	Disadvantages
• Students can refer to the feedback again and again, and continue to learn from it. • Such feedback provides useful evidence for external scrutiny (such as QAA Audit in the UK).	students' work, and hard to make time for when class sizes are large. • You can't refer to your own feedback to different students unless you keep photocopies of their work and your comments. • It becomes tempting to degenerate into shorthand – ticks and crosses – rather than express positive and critical comments.

Word-processed comments

Word-processed comments on each student's assessed work are feedback that you compose, then print out, for each student, summarising your reactions to his or her work. They may be accompanied by an assessment judgement.

Table 21 Advantages and disadvantages of feedback presented via word-processed comments

Advantages	Disadvantages
• Such feedback can remain individual, personal and authoritative. • It is easier to include pre-prepared statements, using 'cut and paste'. • Students can refer to it time and time again. • It is easier to read. • You can keep copies (paper or electronic) and refer to it easily again. • It provides useful evidence for external scrutiny.	• Printed feedback can seem threatening to students when it is critical. • It may appear less personal to students than handwritten feedback. • It is not so easy to link each feedback point to the exact part of the work that caused you to write it. • The 'cut and paste' elements may show up too strongly to external reviewers if they have been used too widely. • It's not so easy to employ *emphasis* in word-processed feedback so that the most important messages stand out from those that are merely routine.

Model answers or solutions, issued with students' marked work

The category of model answers or solutions covers a wide range of feedback aids, including model answers, perhaps supported by 'commentary' notes highlighting principal matters arising from students' work as a whole, worked solutions to calculations or problems, and so on.

Table 22 Advantages and disadvantages of feedback presented via model answers or solutions

Advantages	Disadvantages
• Students can use model answers to revisit their own work in self-assessment mode and can continue to use them as a frame of reference illustrating the standards they are working towards. • Model answers can save you a lot of time writing individual feedback or explanation to students. • They can be issued to students who missed an assignment, or for reference by students who may have been exempted from it. • They constitute useful evidence of standards and expectations, both for students and for external quality reviewers.	• Because model answers or solutions are relatively impersonal, some students will not really engage in comparing their own work to them. • Students who do the assignment equally well overall, but in different ways, may feel that their individuality is not being valued or recognised. • Students may assume that the model answers represent *all* that they need to know about the topic on which the assignment was based. • Students who missed out an important aspect in their own work may not notice the significance of this, and may still need further feedback about their own particular strengths and weaknesses. • If the same assignment is used again within a year or two, there may be clear evidence that the model answers are still in circulation!

Assignment return sheets

Assignment return sheets are normally pre-prepared pro formas on which you provide detailed written or word-processed (or electronic) feedback comments to students on each of a number of assessment criteria applied to their work.

Table 23 Advantages and disadvantages of feedback presented via assessment return sheets

Advantages	Disadvantages
• You can plan to address each of the most important or recurring feedback agendas without having to write out the context, or the relevant criteria, each time. • Students can compare the feedback they receive with that received by peers on the basis of each separate criterion if they wish. • You can copy the assignment return sheets and keep them for your own records (and for external scrutiny) much	• Not all the feedback you wish in practice to give to individual students is likely to relate to the anticipated agendas on an assignment return sheet. • Students may question you about the differences in their scores or grades. • You may have to find other ways to keep for your own records (and for external review) the individual feedback that you add for students. • Any pre-prepared agenda is likely to be found inappropriate for at least some of

Table 23 continued

Advantages	Disadvantages
more easily than you could keep copies of whole assignments along with your written feedback. • The essential parts of the feedback agenda are clarified by the assignment return sheets, giving students a frame of reference for what is expected of them in similar assignments in future. • The elements of the assignment return sheets can be fine-tuned to reflect the intended learning outcomes associated with the assessed work (a feature particularly welcomed by external reviewers seeking connections between assessment criteria and published learning outcomes).	the assignments, for example students who do the assignment very well but in an unanticipated way, or students whose work meets the published agenda but where you feel that they still have not actually understood what they are doing (or suspect that plagiarism has occurred).

Word-processed overall class reports

Word-processes overall class reports on an assignment might be issued to a whole (large) group of students after their work has been marked, along with (or even in advance of) the return to them of their marked work. Ideally, such an overall report can be debriefed in a whole-group session with the students.

Table 24 Advantages and disadvantages of feedback presented via word-processed overall class reports

Advantages	Disadvantages
• Students can look back at the report again and again as necessary. • Students can learn from the feedback on mistakes or inadequacies of *other* students' work, and find out from the report about difficulties that were commonly encountered. • Such reports can save you from having to write repeatedly the same feedback messages in response to commonly occurring mistakes. • Writing such feedback reports causes you to reflect in some detail on overall student performance in the particular assignment concerned, and can show	• Feedback to students is much less personal than is possible using some of the other processes described elsewhere in this book and will tend to concentrate on commonly occurring features in the work of the cohort, perhaps missing out on individuality shown by some of the stronger students. • Students may think that the only important points they need to bear in mind are contained in the report. • If some students are likely to submit their work late, you may need to delay issuing the report (or even have to make further adjustments to it), resulting in the main

Table 24 continued

Advantages	Disadvantages
this to significant others (for example, quality reviewers).	body of students experiencing delay in receiving feedback, and a loss of the 'fresh in mind' dimension when they compare the report with their own work.

Codes written on students' work, debriefed in a class session

For example, instead of writing individual positive or critical comments directly onto students' work, write only a code (a letter, number or symbol), and alongside compile your 'glossary of codes' on overheads, paper or PowerPoint slides, to use when you debrief the work to the whole group (and to issue as a translation device so that students can revisit their work and remind themselves of your feedback).

Table 25 Advantages and disadvantages of feedback presented via codes written on students' work

Advantages	Disadvantages
• Using codes can save you a very significant amount of time and energy when 'hand-marking' a set of assignments, as in principle you only need to spell out each common feedback comment once (in your glossary, rather than on their work). • When addressing common errors or misunderstandings, you can take more time to adjust your feedback messages to make them really understandable. • It is not always possible to squeeze the comment you wish to make to students into the space available between their lines; it's usually much easier to insert a code letter, number or symbol. This means that students see exactly where the feedback comment relates to their own work. • Students get their work back without its being covered with threatening feedback markings. • In your debriefing with the whole group, you can go through each of the important codes one at a time, meaning that all the students to whom the message is directed get the translation	• It is harder for you to remember which students made which misunderstandings or mistakes (unless you photocopy their work with your codes on it, or make some sort of grid recording the codes used for each student). • Students may lose the glossary you issue to them, or may not go to the trouble of retranslating your codes when they review their work later. • The process of debriefing can be boring to the better students who made few of the errors or misunderstandings that you explain to the rest of the cohort. • Poorer students may simply disregard the whole process, especially if they get a lot of code marks on their work.

Table 25 continued

Advantages	Disadvantages
of their code at the same moment. This point-by-point debriefing focuses students' attention much more sharply than when general debriefings are given. For example, until you reveal your message, *all* students with a 'W' written once or more on their work will be trying to work out for themselves what that 'W' might mean. • Students can see that they are not alone in making mistakes. • Students can learn from the mistakes that others have made, but that they have unwittingly avoided this time round. • Students' curiosity makes them check back the comments against the codes, ensuring that they read what you say.	

31

Face-to-face feedback

Face-to-face feedback can carry with it very high learning pay-off for students. It can be memorable, and can help students to change their attitudes and approaches. Face-to-face feedback (whether to individuals or groups) carries with it the additional explanation that comes through body language, facial expression, tone of voice, emphasis, and so on. Furthermore, in face-to-face feedback situations *you* have immediate feedback on how your messages are getting across to students. You can tell a lot about how they are reacting to your feedback from their expressions, body language, and so on. Moreover, you can *adjust* what you say, and how you say it, in response to your observations of what is happening.

Face-to-face feedback to whole classes

Face-to-face feedback can be given orally to a whole class after having marked their assignments, before or after returning their actual work to them. Alternatively, you can give face-to-face feedback to the whole group about the task immediately after collecting their work from them, but before you've marked it, so that they get at least some feedback on the task as soon as possible, while the task is still fresh in their minds.

Table 26 Advantages and disadvantages of face-to-face feedback to whole classes

Advantages	Disadvantages
• You can give a lot of feedback to a lot of students in a relatively short time. • Feedback is strengthened by tone of voice, facial expression, body language, emphasis, and so on. • Students can compare reactions to your feedback, especially when you	• Feedback is less individual, personal and intimate to students. • You can only concentrate on principal feedback matters, and can't cover less common feedback issues. • Students' records or memories of your feedback may be inaccurate and sketchy,

Table 26 continued

Advantages	Disadvantages
use some discussion in the process. • You can support (and partially evidence) giving feedback to the whole group by issuing a handout summarising the main points you include.	and they may not remember the detail when later they look back over their assessed work. • Students may be so busy thinking about one particular aspect of your feedback, which they know will apply to their particular work, that they miss other elements as you talk.

Face-to-face feedback to individual students

Individually given face-to-face feedback can include one-to-one appointments with students, individual discussions out of class or in practical settings, and so on.

Table 27 Advantages and disadvantages of face-to-face feedback to individual students

Advantages	Disadvantages
• Face-to-face feedback one-to-one can bring into sharper focus all the advantages of oral communication: tone of voice, facial expression, body language, emphasis of speech, and so on. This means that the feedback messages can be delivered very clearly in face-to-face contexts, and the learning pay-off associated with the feedback can be very high. • Feedback is likely to be found to be personal, intimate and authoritative. • You can address each individual student's needs, strengths and weaknesses. • It is often much quicker to talk than to write or type. • It is an important feedback mechanism to be able to justify to external reviewers (but of course you'll need evidence to support your claims for it – for example, feedback from students *about* your face-to-face feedback with them).	• One-to-one face-to-face feedback can be perceived as threatening when critical. • Students may become defensive when receiving critical feedback, and you may feel tempted to go in harder to justify the feedback. • Students can be embarrassed when receiving positive feedback, and this can cause them not to fully benefit from praise. • It takes a great deal of time to organise individual appointments with each member of large classes. • There can be even more time wasted between appointments, and with students who don't turn up. • Students often tend to remember only *some* of a feedback interview with an important person like you, often the most critical element, and this may undermine confidence unduly. • When class sizes are large, it becomes impossible to remember exactly what you said to whom.

Face-to-face feedback to small groups of students

Face-to-face feedback given to small groups of students is often timetabled into tutorial sessions, or in group work where students are working on projects or practical tasks. Some of the advantages of face-to-face feedback can be further exploited, and some of the disadvantages of feeding back to individuals are reduced.

Table 28 Advantages and disadvantages of face-to-face feedback to small groups of students

Advantages	Disadvantages
• It can be less threatening to students than one-to-one feedback, especially when critical. • Individuals' needs can be addressed, while still retaining some degree of relative anonymity within the group. • Students can learn from the detail of feedback to others in the group and avoid the problems that others have encountered, and put their own work into context. • You can enter into detailed discussion if the students in the group wish, so that matters arising are followed up in as much depth – often more – as would have happened with individual one-to-one appointments.	• Students may not take quite as much notice of feedback to them as members of a group, than they would have done to one-to-one feedback. • It can be hard to remember to include all the feedback matters which are needed by the group as a whole. • Discussions may get out of perspective, and result in only part of the intended overall feedback agenda being covered by the group session.

32

Electronic feedback

The range and variety of the use of electronic feedback is one of the fastest growth areas in higher education today. Increasingly, tutors are finding that electronic feedback not only speeds up the delivery of feedback and aids the effectiveness of its reception, but also assists with generating appropriate evidence for the quality of feedback.

Emailed comments on students' assessed work

Emailed comments are most often given in the form of one-to-one individual feedback on students' work. The level can range from simple qualitative overall feedback to very detailed comments. An example of the latter is when tutors use the 'Track Changes' facilities of Word, or similar arrangements with other word-processing packages, to return to students their original word-processed assignments duly edited with feedback comments that appear on-screen in another colour. Suggested changes can be electronically 'accepted' or 'rejected' by students using these facilities, and they can produce a post-feedback edition of their work if they wish (or they can be required to do so as part of the overall assessment process).

Table 29 Advantages and disadvantages of feedback presented via emailed comments on students' assessed work

Advantages	Disadvantages
• You can send at any convenient time or place as you're assessing their work. • You have the opportunity to edit your feedback before you finally send it – how often have we (when using handwritten feedback) written quite a lot of feedback down, only to find that the	• Students may have limited access to networked computers, and may be somewhat rushed when they have opportunities to receive your feedback. • Students may not treat your feedback as seriously as if it were face to face, or on printed or handwritten paper.

Table 29 continued

Advantages	Disadvantages
student concerned addressed the point a paragraph or page later!	• Students may not be able to look at your feedback at the same time as their original work (you may still have the latter), or may not take time to look through their returned work and match up your feedback comments with the detail of their work.
• They can receive when they're ready, and usually take in your feedback in the relative comfort of privacy.	
• You can tailor your feedback to individual students' needs, strengths and weaknesses.	
• Students can refer back to your feedback again and again.	• Students are more likely to 'lose' emailed feedback than printed or handwritten feedback.
• You can keep track of what feedback you have given to which students.	
• You can use electronic cut and paste, and save yourself having to type out frequently needed messages more than once.	• Assessors may have difficulty juggling scripts alongside their computers on crowded desks.
• Students can reply directly *about* your feedback.	
• Useful evidence is built up relatively automatically, for external review.	

Computer conferences for overall comments on batches of students' work

Computer conferences provide the option for one-to-many electronic communication for feedback messages that have relevance to the majority of a group of students, along with the chance to go to one-to-one communication for those parts of feedback messages that are more individual or personal.

Table 30 Advantages and disadvantages of feedback presented via computer conferences

Advantages	Disadvantages
• Just about all the advantages of emailed feedback still apply, except the option of responding individually through the conference to each student's strengths and weaknesses. Even this can, of course, be addressed by adding individualised emails to the computer conference communication.	• Students may be less inclined to search through a generalised electronic feedback message for elements that apply to their own work.
	• Students replying to the conference about your feedback may feel more exposed than when replying directly to you by email. (Of course there is no reason why you should deny them private communication.)
• Your overall feedback response to an assignment can be sent as it stands to each of many students, who can each	• Students with less developed information

Table 30 continued

Advantages	Disadvantages
receive it when and where it is convenient to them. • You can save time responding to matters affecting many students, and use some of the time saved to reply separately by email to those students needing more detailed or individual feedback. • Students can learn from your feedback to issues *other* than the ones that they themselves need to think about. • Students can reply individually to you about your overall feedback, and (if you structure the conference accordingly) can directly see each other's responses to your feedback, and generate real conference-type discussion of matters arising from an assignment (and from your own assessment of and feedback concerning the assignment).	technology literacy may not participate as actively in computer conferences as do their more computer-literate colleagues.

Computer-delivered feedback

The broad category of computer-delivered feedback includes the use of (pre-prepared) feedback responses to structured self-assessment questions in computer-based learning packages. Computer-based feedback can be programmed into learning packages on floppy disk or CD-ROM, and can also be programmed into Web-based packages delivered through intranets or the Internet.

Table 31 Advantages and disadvantages of computer-delivered feedback

Advantages	Disadvantages
• Students can work through computer-based learning materials at their own pace, and, within limits, at their own choice of time and place. • Feedback to pre-designed tasks can be received almost instantly by students at the point of entering their decision or choice into the system. • Computer-based feedback legitimises learning by trial and error, and allows	• You cannot easily tell to what extent individual students are benefiting from the feedback you have designed. • Students who don't understand the feedback responses you have designed may not be able to question you further at the time in the ways they could have done with emailed or computer conference-based feedback. • The 'now you see it, now it's gone' syndrome can affect students' retention

Table 31 continued

Advantages	Disadvantages
students to learn from mistakes in the comfort of privacy. • You can prepare detailed feedback in anticipation of the most likely mistakes or misconceptions that you know will be common among your students. • Students can view the feedback as often as they need it as they work through the package.	of your feedback messages, as students move quickly from one screenful of information to another in the package. • Technophobes may find the medium gets in the way of the message.

Tips on giving electronic feedback

Computer communications are very fast and cheap, so they are very useful for providing feedback to students. Email is particularly useful as a vehicle for giving students individual feedback on assessed work, whether as stand-alone email communications to students or alongside or within a computer conferencing system. Electronic feedback can apply to computer-mediated coursework (where the work is submitted through a computer system), but can also extend usefully to giving students feedback on handwritten or hard-copy work that they have submitted for assessment. The following suggestions may help you to exploit the benefits of communications technology, not least to save your own time and energy in giving students feedback.

1 **Acknowledge receipt of assessments.** Students will be worried that their work hasn't arrived safely, so tell them when it has arrived. An email message is best for this, because it is private.

2 **Provide specific feedback to individuals by email.** As this method of communication is private, it is suitable for giving comments on work to individuals. It is much easier to write this kind of communication by computer than by hand, so use the technology for the whole process.

3 **Investigate word processing software to help with assessment of written work.** If work is produced by word processing, it is often possible to add comments to it. You can use this to provide comments on the work as part of the feedback process.

4 **Encourage students to send you assessments or samples of work as email attachments.** If work is being produced on a computer, it is easy and quick to attach a saved file to an email message. It will arrive very quickly and it is very cheap to send it.

125

5   **Make the most of the comfort of privacy.** When students receive feedback by email (as opposed to face to face or in group situations), they have the comfort of being able to read the feedback without anyone (particularly you!) being able to see their reactions to it. This is most useful when you need to give students some critical feedback.

6   **Remember that you can edit your own feedback before you send it.** For example, you may well want to adjust individual feedback comments in the light of students' overall performance. It is much harder to edit hand-written feedback on students' written work. Email feedback allows you to type in immediate feedback concerning things that you see in each student's work, and to adjust or delete particular parts of your feedback as you go further into marking their work.

7   **Exploit the space.** Inserting handwritten feedback comments into students' written work is limited by the amount of space that there may be for your comments. With email feedback, you don't have to restrict your wording if you need to elaborate on a point.

8   **Consider combining email feedback with written feedback.** For example, you can write onto students' work a series of numbers or letters at the points where you wish to give detailed feedback. The email feedback can then translate these numbers or letters into feedback comments or phrases, so that students can see exactly what each element of feedback is telling them. The fact that students then have to decode each feedback element helps them to think about it more deeply, and learn from it more effectively, than when they can see the feedback directly on their work.

9   **Spare yourself from repeated typing.** When designing computer-delivered feedback messages, you should only have to type each message once. You can then copy and paste all the messages in cases when you need to give several students the same feedback information. It can be useful to combine this process with numbers or letters that you write onto students' work, building up each email to individual students by pasting together the feedback messages that go with each of the numbers or letters.

10 **Consider the possibilities of 'global' feedback messages.** For example, you may wish to give all the students in a large group the same feedback message about overall matters arising from a test or exercise. The overall message can be pasted into each email, before the individual comments addressed to each student.

11 **Check that your email feedback is getting through.** Most email systems can be programmed to send you back a message saying when the email was opened, and by whom. This can help you to identify any students who are

not opening their emails. It can also be useful to end each email with a question asking the student to reply to you on some point arising from the feedback. This helps to make sure that students don't just open their email feedback messages, but have to read them!

12   **Keep records of your email feedback.** It is easy to keep copies on disk of all of your feedback to each student, and you can open a folder for each student if you wish. This makes it much easier to keep track of your ongoing feedback to individual students than does giving handwritten feedback that is lost to you when you return their work to them.

13   **Make the most of the technology.** For example, many email systems support spell-check facilities, which can allow you to type really fast and ignore most of the resulting errors, then correct them all just before sending your message. This also causes you to re-read each message, which can be very useful for encouraging you to add second thoughts that may have occurred to you as you went further in your assessment of the task.

14   **Use email to gather feedback from your students.** Students are often bolder sitting at a computer terminal than they are face to face. Ask your students questions about how they are finding selected aspects of their studies, but don't turn it into an obvious routine questionnaire. Include some open-ended questions so that they feel free to let you know how they are feeling about their own progress, and about your teaching too.

15   **Use a computer conference to provide subtle pressure on students to submit work on time.** Publish lists of work you have received from students, but without names. This will make those who haven't submitted work realise that they could be falling behind.

16   **Create a new conference topic for discussion of each assessment.** Students may want to exchange ideas after they have received feedback on assessed work. If you provide a topic for this, they will know where to discuss this without affecting the structure of the rest of the conference.

17   **Seek permission from participants to use their work to give general feedback to the group.** If the work of one of the students includes something that you could use to illustrate a point useful to the whole group, ask their permission to use it. An email message is the appropriate medium to use for this: the work could remain anonymous. Once you have permission, you can copy the appropriate sections to the conference and discuss it there.

18   **Use the conference system to provide general feedback to groups.** When you are assessing work, there will be common points that need to be

raised for several people. If these are discussed on the group's conference without naming anybody, participants can learn from each other's mistakes.

19   **Consider putting assessment statistics on the conference.** You could make some basic information (such as average scores) available to the group. Some people might find it helpful to see how their performance compared with that of others in the group. On the other hand, some people might find this demoralising, so this issue needs careful thought.

20   **Manage students' expectations.** Don't start by giving too much feedback to students, or they will expect similar amounts of feedback every time. Be clear about how much feedback it is reasonable for you to give to each student, and how often you can do this.

Using computer-generated feedback

Human beings can get bored when giving the same feedback repeatedly to different students; computers don't have this problem! Computer-generated feedback involves programming the feedback messages you wish students to receive in anticipated circumstances, such as replying to options in multiple-choice questions.

1   **Look for those occasions where you frequently need to give the same feedback message to different students.** Work out exactly what the gist of your feedback message is on such occasions and consider whether it is worth packaging up this feedback so that students can get the same help from a computer instead of from you.

2   **Listen to yourself giving live feedback to students after they have attempted a task.** It can be worth tape-recording some examples of the way you talk to fellow human beings. The little 'asides' that you slip in to make sure they understand you are very important, and it's worth incorporating such asides in the feedback you get the computer to give them.

3   **Devise a task leading towards the planned feedback message.** Normally the feedback will be reserved for those students who don't get the task right first time. Check out with live students that the planned feedback is self-sufficient, and that they don't need any further explanation from you in person to get the task right next time.

4   **Don't forget to provide feedback to students who get the task *right* first time.** It is just as important to give positive feedback for successful work as it is to give helpful feedback when students encounter problems. Remind them exactly *what* they got right, in case it was a lucky accident.

5   **Let students who get things right know about some of the things that might have gone wrong.** Learning from mistakes is useful, and people who don't make any mistakes can miss out on some valuable learning. Students are often quite hooked on finding out more about what they *might* have done wrong, even when they got it all right, and will search for what the computer would have told them if they had got it wrong.

6   **Be sympathetic to students who get it wrong.** When you program feedback into a computer-based learning package, it is important that your students feel that the computer is treating them like human beings. Don't include blunt messages such as 'Wrong!' or 'Wrong yet again!' It is better to come across almost apologetically, with feedback messages starting perhaps as 'Sorry, but this doesn't work out in practice . . .'

7   **Remind students about *what* they get wrong.** It is important that mistakes can be linked firmly to the task that brought them about. The danger is that when your students read your feedback messages, as programmed into the computer system, they may have forgotten exactly what they were trying to do when things went wrong.

8   **Try to devise feedback that explains *why* students may have got something wrong.** It isn't enough just to know *what* was wrong. Whenever you can, devise feedback messages about mistakes along the lines 'For this to have happened, you may have been thinking that . . . , but in fact it's like this . . .'.

9   **Test out your feedback messages with small groups of students.** Ask them if they can think of any better ways of getting the feedback message across. Get them to put into words what *they* might have said to someone sitting next to them who attempted the same task and got it wrong. If their words are better than your original ones, use theirs!

10 **Explore the possibilities of using email for 'later' feedback.** When you know how well (or badly) students have tackled a computer-based exercise, you may be able to give them feedback through the system of networked computers. This means that only the students concerned see these particular feedback message, and they have the comfort of privacy in which to read the feedback and think about it.

Chapter 5

Involving students in their own assessment

33 Why consider student peer assessment?
34 What lends itself to peer assessment?
35 Getting started with peer assessment
36 Getting students to formulate criteria
37 Student self-assessment
38 Setting up self-assessment tutor dialogues
39 Further questions to elicit reflection
40 Yet more questions to promote reflection

33

Why consider student peer assessment?

Nothing affects students more than assessment, yet they often claim that they are in the dark as to what goes on in the minds of their assessors and examiners. Involving students in peer assessment and self-assessment can let them into the assessment culture they must survive. Increasingly, peer assessment is being used to involve students more closely in their learning and its evaluation, and to help to enable students really understand what is required of them. It is not a 'quick fix' solution to reduce staff marking time, as it is intensive in its use of lecturer time at the briefing and development stages. It can have enormous benefits in terms of learning gain.

Introducing student peer assessment can seem a daunting and hazardous prospect if you're surrounded by an assessment culture in which lecturers undertake all the assessing. There are, however, several good reasons why the prospect should not be seen as so formidable, including the following.

1   **Students are doing it already.** Students are continuously peer-assessing, in fact. One of the most significant sources of answers to students' pervading question 'How am I doing?' is the feedback they get about their own learning achievements and performances by comparing them with those of others. It is true that feedback from tutors is regarded as more authoritative, but there is less such feedback available from tutors than from fellow learners. Setting up and facilitating peer assessment therefore legitimises and makes respectable something that most students are already engaged in.

2   **Students find out more about our assessment cultures.** One of the biggest dangers with assessment is that students often don't really know how their assessment works. They often approach both exams and tutor-marked coursework as if they were black holes that they might be sucked into! Getting involved in peer assessment makes the assessment culture much more transparent, and students gain a better idea of exactly what will be expected of them in their efforts to demonstrate their achievement of the intended learning outcomes.

3   **We can't do as much assessing as we used to do.** With more students, heavier teaching loads and shorter timescales (sometimes caused by moves to modularisation and semesterisation), the amount of assessment that lecturers can cope with is limited. While it is to be hoped that our assessment will still be valid, fair and reliable, it remains the case that the amount of feedback to students that lecturers can give is less per capita. Peer assessment, when facilitated well, can be a vehicle for getting much more feedback to students.

4   **Students learn more deeply when they have a sense of ownership of the agenda.** When peer assessment is employed using assessment criteria that are devised by the students themselves, the sense of ownership of the criteria helps them to apply their criteria much more objectively than when they are applying tutors' criteria to each other's work.

5   **The act of assessing is one of the deepest learning experiences.** Applying criteria to someone else's work is one of the most productive ways of developing and deepening understanding of the subject matter involved in the process. 'Measuring' and 'judging' are far more rigorous processes than simply reading, listening or watching.

6   **Peer assessment allows students to learn from each other's successes.** Students involved in peer assessment cannot fail to take notice of instances where the work they are assessing is in some way better than their own efforts. When this process of learning from each other is legitimised and encouraged, students can benefit a great deal from the work of the most able in the group.

7   **Peer assessment allows students to learn from each other's weaknesses.** Students peer-assessing are likely to discover all sorts of mistakes that they did not make themselves. This can be really useful for them, as their awareness of 'what not to do' increases, and they become much less likely to fall into traps that might otherwise have caused them problems in their future work.

34

What lends itself to peer assessment?

Almost anything that can be assessed can also be peer-assessed. The list that follows includes some pointers about why it can be useful to employ peer assessment in various contexts.

1   **Student presentations.** Peer assessment is particularly useful for the style and process dimensions of student presentations. It can also be used for the content side of presentations when the topics are sufficiently shared that students are well informed enough to make judgements on the content of each other's presentations.

2   **Reports.** Peer assessment helps to alert students to good and bad practice in report-writing, and helps them develop awareness of the importance of structure, coherence and layout in reports.

3   **Essay plans.** Peer assessment of essay plans can widen students' horizons about different ways of brainstorming the content and structure of essays. It takes almost as much creative thinking to design the content of an essay plan as it would to produce the final essay, so peer-assessing such plans helps students to cover a lot of sharing of ideas in a relatively short time.

4   **Calculations.** Peer-assessing correct answers is simple and quick. Peer assessment allows students to identify exactly where things went wrong when they are marking incorrect answers, and alerts students to potential trouble spots to avoid in the future.

5   **Interviews.** Peer assessment allows students to exchange a range of opinions, attitudes and reactions to each other's interview performance in a less threatening way than can be the case when such performance is assessed by the lecturer.

6 **Annotated bibliographies.** Peer assessment of bibliographies can be a fast and effective way of alerting students to *other* sources of reference that, working on their own, they might have overlooked.

7 **Practical work.** Peer assessment of experimental work can allow students to receive feedback on their practical skills, whereas lecturer assessment of such skills may be threatening – or not possible (for example, owing to limited assessor availability when large groups of students are involved).

8 **Poster displays.** Peer assessment of poster displays can be a rapid way of alerting students to a wide range of approaches to the visual presentation of ideas.

9 **Portfolios.** In cases when students are familiar with all the requirements for the successful demonstration of their achievements through portfolios, they are often highly competent in assessing each other's, particularly if they themselves have recently undertaken a similar preparation task.

10 **Exhibitions and artefacts.** Art students in particular have a long tradition of participating in critiques of each other's paintings, plans, models, garments, sculptures, and so on. Students participating in 'crits' learn a lot about the level of work required and the ways in which aesthetic judgements of work are formed within their own particular subject contexts.

11 **Performances.** Students can learn a great deal about their own performing skills by assessing each other's performances. Peer assessment additionally helps them to tune in to the sorts of criteria that are used by official 'judges' when assessing performances, and opens up the possibility of a great deal of useful feedback about both the performances themselves, and the interpretation and application of the relevant assessment criteria.

35

Getting started with peer assessment

1 **Take it a bit at a time.** Some people (students and lecturers) find the use of peer assessment very radical, so it is a good idea to introduce it gradually, on a small scale, until you, your colleagues and your students are confident about how it will work best.

2 **Keep everyone in the picture.** Tell everyone what you are doing and why. Students and colleagues need to understand the thinking behind what you are doing, to avoid their perceiving it as a soft option or abdication of responsibility. If they understand that peer assessment is actually part of the learning process, they may find it more acceptable.

3 **Provide mark-free rehearsal opportunities.** This helps students get the hang of what is required of them, and also builds in an opportunity for students to get interim feedback at a stage when there is time to bring about improvements.

4 **Provide, or negotiate, really clear assessment criteria.** If the criteria are unambiguous and explicit, students should not be able to over-mark friends or penalise enemies. All marks should be justifiable by reference to the criteria, and to the evidence of achievement of them.

5 **Make peer assessment marks meaningful.** Some argue that peer review is really only suitable for feedback purposes. However, if students are to take peer assessment seriously, it should count for something, even if only a small proportion of the final grade. You may prefer to parallel-mark, with assessor grades counting as well as averaged peer grades if this is appropriate.

6 **Moderate peer assessment.** To ensure that the students see peer assessment as fair, lecturers must overview the marks awarded and provide a 'court of appeal' if students feel justice has not been done. This may mean offering vivas to any dissatisfied candidates.

7   **Keep the system simple.** Try not to give yourself really complicated addition and averaging tasks to do after peer assessment has taken place. Too many separate components make it laborious to arrive at final marks. If the numerical side can't be simplified, it is worth using computer programs to do the donkey work!

8   **Involve students in the assessment criteria.** You can do this by letting students participate in the generation of assessment criteria, and the weighting to be given to each criterion. Alternatively, you can provide the criteria in the first instance and give students lots of opportunities to ask questions about what they really mean.

9   **Allow plenty of time.** Just because *you* can assess a poster display or an essay fairly quickly doesn't mean that students will be able to do so too, especially if groups are assessing other groups and are required to provide a mark by consensus. Presentations *always* overrun, and students will tend to reach snap conclusions and make 'guesstimates' when under pressure regarding time.

10 **Monitor student achievement.** It's a good idea to review how well students are peer-assessing, by the same kinds of methods you may use to review your own assessment, to ensure reliability and validity of marking. It is often reassuring for students (and colleagues) to see that peer assessment using explicit criteria, and based on the production of clearly specified evidence, produces data that are very similar to marks produced by lecturers themselves.

36

Getting students to formulate criteria

As has been mentioned already, peer assessment works at its best when students own the assessment criteria. Furthermore, it is important that the criteria are clearly understood by all the students, and that their understanding is shared. The best way of developing a set of good criteria is to involve the students in the process from the outset. It is crucial not to put words in students' mouths during this process, otherwise the assessment agenda can revert to academic terminology that students don't understand. The following processes can be used to generate a set of peer assessment criteria 'from scratch'.

The processes described in this section can be adapted to helping students to generate their own peer assessment criteria for any of a wide range of tasks, but the discussion that follows focuses on students preparing to peer-assess presentations. However, parallel steps can be used for generating student-owned assessment criteria for 'an essay', 'a report', 'a poster display', 'an interview', 'an annotated bibliography', 'a student-devised exam paper', and countless other assessment possibilities.

It is possible to go through all the processes listed here with a group of over 100 students in less than an hour. The more often you do this with students, the faster and better you will become at it (and at taking short cuts where appropriate, or tailoring the steps to your own subject, and to the particular students, and so on).

In practice, you are very unlikely to need to build in all 18 of the steps outlined in the following list in any given instance of negotiating criteria with a group of students. Usually, at least some of the processes may be skipped, but it is worth thinking through the implications of all the stages before making your own decision about which are most relevant to the particular conditions under which you are planning to facilitate peer assessment.

1   **Brainstorming:** Ask all students to jot down individually a few key words in response to the question 'What makes a really *good* 10-minute presentation? Jot down some of the things you would look for in an excellent example of one.'

2   **Sharing:** Get students to work in groups. Even in a large lecture theatre they can work in groups of four or five with their near neighbours. Alternatively, if students are free to move around the room where the exercise is happening, they can be put into random groups (alphabetically, or by birthday month, or they can be allowed to form self-selecting groups). Ask the groups to share and discuss for a few minutes *all* their ideas concerning a good presentation.

3   **Prioritising:** Ask the groups to make a shortlist of (say) 'the most important *five* features of a good 10-minute presentation'. Ask each group to appoint a scribe to note down the shortlist.

4   **Editing:** Get the groups to look carefully at the wording of each item on their shortlists. For example, tell them that when they report back an item from their list, if you can't tell exactly what it means, you will ask them to tell you 'what it *really* means is . . .'. Maybe mention that some of the more academic words such as 'coherence', 'structure' and 'delivery' may need some translation into everyday words (maybe along the lines of 'hangs well together, one point following on logically to the next' , 'good interest-catching opening, logical order for the middle, and firm solid conclusion' and 'clearly spoken, well illustrated, backed up by facts or figures'). However, don't put too many words of any kind into students' minds; let them think of their own words.

5   **Reprioritising:** Remind the groups about the shortlisting process, and to get their five features into order of priority. This may have changed during the editing process as meanings became clearer.

6   **Turning features into checklist questions:** Suggest that the groups now edit each of their features into a question format – for example, 'Was there a good finish?', 'How well was the material researched?', and so on. The point of this is to pave the way for a checklist of criteria that will be more straightforward as a basis for making judgements.

7   **Collecting the most important questions in the room:** Now start collecting 'top' feature questions. Ask each group in turn for the thing that came top of its list. Write these up one at a time on a flip chart or overhead transparency, so that the whole class can see the emerging list of criteria. Where one group's highest-rating point is very similar to one that has already been given, either put a tick beside the original one (to acknowledge that the same point has been rated as important by more than one group), or (better) adjust the wording slightly so that the flip-charted criterion reflects *both* the sources equally. Continue this process until each of the groups has reported its top criterion.

8   **Fleshing out the agenda:** Now go back round the groups (in reverse order) asking for 'the second most important thing on your list'. At this stage, the overlaps begin to occur thick and fast, but there will still emerge new and different checklist questions based on further features identified by the groups. Use ticks (maybe in a different colour from the overlaps of top-rated questions) to make the degree of concurrence visible to the whole group as the picture continues to unfold. With a large class you may need to use more than one flip-chart sheet (or overhead transparency), but it is important to try to keep all of the agenda that is unfolding visible to the whole class. This means posting up filled flip charts where everyone can see them, or alternating the transparencies so that students remember what has already come up.

9   **Any other business?** If the degree of overlap has increased significantly, and, after all the second-round contributions have been gained, the flow of new ideas has slowed down, it is worth asking the whole group for 'any fairly important things that still aren't represented on your list'. Usually there will be a further two or three significant contributions at this stage.

10   **Numbering the agenda:** When all the criteria questions have been noted down, *number them*. Simply write numbers beside each criterion in the order in which they were given. During this stage, if you notice that two criteria are more or less the same, it can be worth asking the class whether you can clump them together.

11   **Weighting individually:** Next, ask students to work individually again. Ask them to weight each criterion, using an agreed total number of marks. Choosing the total number needs care! If there are ten criteria, 100 marks would be too tempting because some students would probably just give each criterion ten marks, thereby avoiding the real business of making prioritising decisions. Thirteen criteria and 60 marks works better, for example. Ask every student to ensure that the total marks number adds up to the agreed figure. Allow students to ignore any criteria that they individually don't think are important: 'If you think it's irrelevant, just score it zero.'

12   **Recording everyone's weighting publicly:** The next stage is to record everyone's marks on the flip charts or transparencies. This means starting with criterion number 1 and writing beneath it *everyone's* marks rating. It's worth establishing a reporting-back order round the room first, so that every student knows who to follow (and encouraging students to nudge anyone who has lost concentration and is failing to give you a score!). Saying, 'Can you shout them out as fast as I can write them up?' usually keeps everyone (including you) working at speed.

13   **Optional separating:** It can be worth starting with two flip charts from the outset. For example, you may wish to record separately the criteria relating

to *content* and those relating to *structure*. This may pave the way for peer assessment grids that help to separate such dimensions.

14 **Discussing divergent views:** Then go through all of the remaining criteria in the same way. Don't worry that, sometimes, consecutive scores for the same criterion will be quite divergent. When this happens, it will be a rich agenda for discussion later, and if you're writing the scores up in the same order each time, it's not too hard to pinpoint the particular individual who gave an unusually high or low rating to any criterion. You can, for example, ask the student who rated criterion 8 highest to argue briefly with the student who rated it lowest, and see what the causes of the divergence may be.

15 **Averaging:** Next, average out all the scores. If there are students with calculators in the group, the average rating may be forthcoming from the group without any prompting. Otherwise, it's usually possible to do some averaging and rounding up or down to the nearest whole number just intuitively by looking at the numbers. Ask the whole group, 'Does criterion 7 get a 5 or a 6 please? Hands up those who make it a 5', and so on.

16 **Shedding weak criteria:** Look back at the whole range of criteria and ratings. At this point there will usually be one or more criteria that can safely be dropped from the agenda. They may have seemed like a good idea at the time to some of the students, but the visible ratings tell their own story.

17 **Confirming ownership:** 'Are you all happy to proceed with the averaged out version of the ratings, and with these criteria?' is the question to ask next. Mostly, there will be no dissent. Just occasionally, a student with a different view of the ratings may wish to speak out against the consensus. It is worth then offering the chance for any individuals who feel strongly about the ratings to choose to be peer-assessed by their own idiosyncratic rating scales, but make it clear that these must now be shared with the whole group for approval. Students rarely wish to do this, particularly if the feeling of ownership of the set of weighted criteria is strong in the group as a whole.

18 **Administrating:** Turn the criteria questions into a grid, with the criteria down the left-hand side and the weighting numbers in a column alongside them, with spaces for students to write in their peer assessment ratings. If students are going to be asked to peer-assess several instances of the task involved (for example, maybe ten short presentations), the grids could be marked up so that students used the same grid for the successive presentations (see Figure 3). Alternatively, if the peer assessment grids are going to be used for a small number of assessments (for example, where all students mark three essays or reports, and each of theirs is to be marked by three other

students), it is worth having separate sheets with a column for individual feedback comments relating to the score awarded for each of the criteria (see Figure 4).

The list of processes given in this section may appear daunting, but in fact it is quite a lot easier to do in practice than it is to write out a description of it! Also, some of the steps are very quick to do. Furthermore, as the culture of peer assessment becomes better known to students, they themselves become better at generating and weighting criteria, and more skilled at applying them well.

Peer assessment grid										
Your name: Date: Session:										
Peer assessment of presentations A to H:	**Mark out of:**	A	B	C	D	E	F	G	H
Is the opening of the presentation strong and clear? Are the intended outcomes of the presentation set out well, whether orally, on slides or on accompanying handout material?	5								
Does the presentation proceed smoothly, so that one point leads naturally to the next?	10								
Are slides or overheads clear, readable and professional in appearance? Are they used well during the presentation?	5								
Is the oral side of the presentation well done? For example, is the voice clear and audible? Does the presenter appear confident and authoritative?	5								
Has the content of the presentation been well-prepared? Is there evidence of sufficient background reading and research? Are sources referred to well on slides and/or handout materials?	5								
How well does the presentation keep to the allotted time? Does it avoid rushing to get everything in towards the end of the time?	5								
How well did the presenter finish the presentation? For example, were the main points summarised well at the end?	5								
How confidently did the presenter answer questions arising from the presentation?	10								
Total	50								

Figure 3 Example of a grid where students peer-assess presentations A to H

Peer assessment with feedback: written task, for example an essay

Your name: Date: Session:

Example being assessed:	Mark	Score	Feedback comments
How good is the abstract? Does the abstract give a realistic summary of the content of the essay, or the way that the essay will address the question?	5		
How well does the essay itself begin? Is it clear how the essay will address the question?	5		
How readable and fluent is the essay? Does the meaning of each idea come across clearly?	10		
How good is the content of the essay? Does it show good evidence of reading and research?	10		
How well are sources cited and referenced? Are sufficient sources referred to? Have the sources been appropriately chosen?	10		
Are arguments presented convincingly and persuasively?	6		
How well does the essay conclude? Does it return to the task or question and summarise the findings or views presented?	10		
How well, overall, does the essay address the particular question or task? For example, does the author present his/her own view, or decision, or ideas?	10		
How well does the essay keep to the suggested word limit? E.g. within 10% = full marks, around 20% half-marks, outside 30% no marks for this element of assessment.	4		
How good are grammar, punctuation, spelling and so on?	10		
Total	80	80	

Figure 4 Grid for individual peer assessments: written task, for example an essay

37

Student self-assessment

There are many levels on which student self-assessment may be used, ranging from activities intended simply to promote reflective learning, to formal strategies that allow students' self-assessment to count in their overall marks. The following suggestions may help you decide when to introduce elements of student self-assessment into your courses.

1   **Make self-assessment an integral element of learning.** Help students to become lifelong learners who can evaluate their own performance after they have finished formal study. This is a valuable skill that will help them in their professional careers.

2   **Consider what no one but students can really assess.** For example, students alone can give a rating to how much effort they put into a task, how strong their motivation is in a particular subject, or how much they believe they have improved at something over a period of time.

3   **Give students practice at positively evaluating themselves.** For example, give them nine Post-it™ notes and ask them to list nine qualities or skills they have, and get them to prioritise them in a ranking order of 1 to 9.

4   **Emphasise the crucial relationship between criteria, evidence and self-evaluation.** Help students to learn to make balanced judgements about themselves that relate directly to the assessment criteria by providing clear evidence of what has been achieved.

5   **Encourage the use of reflective accounts and journals to promote self-evaluation.** If you encourage students to review their own performance regularly through keeping journals, they can build up a picture of their own work over a period of time.

6   **Support students in self-assessment.** Give them lots of guidance at the outset, then progressively let them take a greater degree of responsibility for their assessment as their understanding of the process matures.

7   **Help students to get to grips with assessment criteria.** Let them discuss what the criteria will mean in practice, and get them to describe exactly what sorts of performance or evidence will demonstrate achievement of the criteria.

8   **Help students to prepare for self-assessment by having them assess peers.** It is often easier for students to make judgements about their own work when they have participated in looking critically at what others have done.

9   **Include self-assessment when assessing group process.** Frequently, students are asked to peer-assess each other's contribution to group tasks. It is also feasible for them to assess realistically what they themselves have added to the process, applying the same notions of criteria and evidence as they did to the work of their peers.

10 **Use flexible learning materials.** Most such materials include a lot of self-assessment exercises in one way or another. Usually, the primary benefit of these is not strictly self-assessment, but the delivery of feedback to students who have had a try at the exercises. However, flexible learning continuously develops students' own picture of their progress.

11 **Provide computer-based self-assessment opportunities for students.** It can help students to find out a lot about how their learning is going when computer-based packages are available in a library or resource room, enabling them to check their knowledge in the comfort of privacy. Check out Web sites that could serve a similar purpose for your students. Such packages can also provide feedback and direction, as well as giving students a quantitative indication of the state of their learning.

12 **Provide self-assessment opportunities as diagnostic aids.** Open-learning or computer-based packages can include sets of questions designed to help students identify which sections of their work may need particular attention. The packages can also include remedial 'loops' that students experiencing particular difficulties can be routed through.

13 **Use self-assessment to establish existing competence.** Self-assessment exercises and tests can be a quick way of enabling students to establish how much of their prior learning is relevant to the prerequisite knowledge for their next course or module. This can help students avoid wasting time studying things they have already achieved well enough.

14 **Use self-assessment sometimes in lectures and tutorials.** For example, when students have brought along coursework expecting to hand it in for tutor marking, it can be useful to lead the whole group through self-assessment against clear marking guidelines. The work can still be handed in, and it is usually much faster and easier to moderate students' own assessments than to mark the work from scratch.

15 **Use self-assessment as part of learning contracts.** When students are producing evidence specifically relating to their own learning contracts, it can be useful to ask them to self-assess how well they have demonstrated their achievement of some of their intended outcomes. One way of firming this up is to allocate some tutor-assessed marks for the quality of their own self-assessment; students can be given feedback on this too.

16 **Suggest that students use video to informally self-assess their presentation skills.** Watching video tapes of their own presentations in the comfort of privacy can allow students to reflect very deeply on their skills. In fact, it is sometimes useful to suggest that students view each other's videos informally after self-assessing, to put the self-critical evaluations some students may have made of themselves into more comfortable perspective.

17 **Include self-assessment with student portfolios.** Ask students to include in their portfolios self-evaluations of their work. Reserve some of the marks for portfolios for the quality and depth of students' self-appraisal.

18 **Experiment with non-print media for self-assessment.** For example, when art students are preparing an exhibition or display, ask them to provide an interim self-critique on audio tape.

19 **Get students to self-assess added value.** Getting students to self-appraise the added value that a course or module has given them can be a useful adjunct to student feedback procedures, and helps students to put their learning into perspective in the overall context of their development.

38

Setting up self-assessment tutor dialogues

Think of the following scenario. A piece of coursework is to be handed in and tutor-assessed. This could be just about anything – perhaps a practical report, a fieldwork report, a dissertation, or even an essay or set of answers based on a problems sheet.

Imagine that students are briefed to self-assess their efforts at the point of submitting the work for tutor assessment, and are supplied with a pro forma, of no more than two pages' length, for this self-assessment. Suppose that the pro forma consists of a dozen or so short, structured questions, asking students to make particular reflective comments upon the work they are handing in, and that the principal purposes behind these questions are to:

- get students to reflect on what they have done;

- give tutors assessing their work additional information about 'where each student is' in relation to the tasks they have just attempted;

- form a productive agenda to help tutors to focus their feedback most usefully;

- save tutors time by helping them to avoid telling students things about their submitted work that they know all too clearly already;

- give students a sense of ownership of the most important elements of feedback that they are going to receive on the work they have submitted.

Some ideas for self-assessment agendas

Each of the suggestions that follow could take the form of a relatively small box on the pro forma, requiring students to give their own reply to the question but allowing space for tutors to add a sentence or two in response to each student's reply. Sometimes, of course, tutors would wish to (or need to) enclose additional response information on separate sheets – often pre-prepared handout materials dealing with anticipated problem areas or frequently made errors. A reminder: the menu of questions that follows is exactly that – a menu – from which individual assessors will need to select carefully only a few questions: those that are most relevant to the nature of the assessed task. Also, for every separate task it is vitally important that the self-assessment questionnaires are patently task specific, and that students *don't* see the same (or similar) questionnaires more than once. (We all know how 'surface' students' responses become to repetitively used course evaluation questionnaires, and how limited is the value of the feedback we receive from such instruments!)

For each of the questions included here, we've added a sentence or two about *why* or *when* that question may prove useful to assessors and students. Some parts of the menu are much more 'obvious' than others, and we believe it is among the less common questions that will be found those most likely to set up deep tutor–student dialogue.

1 **What do you honestly consider will be a fair score or grade for the work you are handing in?** Most students are surprisingly good at estimating the worth of their work. Only those students who are more than 5 per cent out (or one grade point) need any detailed feedback on any differences between the actual scores and their own estimates – this saves tutors time.

2 **What do you think was the thing you did best in this assignment?** The fact is that assessors know soon enough what students actually did best, but that's not the same as knowing what they *think* they have done well. Where both are the same thing, there's no need for any response from assessors, but on the occasions where students did something else much better (or did the original thing quite poorly), feedback is vital, and very useful to students.

3 **What did you find the hardest part of this assignment?** Assessors know soon enough what students do least well, but that's not always the thing they found hardest. When a student cites something that was completely mastered – in other words, the assignment gives no clue that this was a struggle – it is essential that he or she is congratulated on the achievement involved – for example, a few words such as 'you say you found this hard, but you've completely cracked it – well done!' go a long way.

4 **If you had the chance to do this assignment again from scratch, how (if at all) might you decide to go about it differently?** This question can save assessors hours! Students usually know what is wrong with the approach they have engaged in. Let them tell you about this! This saves you having to go on at length telling them about it. Moreover, when students themselves have diagnosed the weaknesses in their approach, the ownership of the potential changes in approach lies with them, rather than our having to take control of this.

5   **How difficult (or easy) did you find this assignment?** Don't use number scales! Provide words or phrases that students can underline or ring. Use student language, such as 'dead easy', 'tough in parts', 'straightforward', 'a real pain', 'took longer than it was worth', 'hard but helped me learn' and so on.

6   **What was the most important thing that you learned about the subject through doing this assignment?** Answers to this question give us a lot of information about the extent to which the assignment is delivering learning pay-off to students.

7   **What was the most important thing that you learned about *yourself* while doing this assignment?** Such a question gives us information about how well (or badly) the assignment may be contributing to students' development of key transferable skills, including the skill of self-organisation.

8   **What do you think are the most important things I am looking for in this assignment?** This question can be sobering for assessors – it can show us how students perceive our activities, and it can often show us a lot about how we are found to be assessing. Students can benefit from feedback on their responses when their perceptions of the purposes of an assignment have gone adrift.

9   **To what extent has doing this assignment changed your opinions?** Not all assignments have anything to do with developing students' views, attitudes or opinions, but some do this, and it is important that we acknowledge this when such issues are intentional. Such a question is better than simply asking, 'Has your opinion changed?', where the expectation is clearly for a 'yes' response.

10 **What's the worst paragraph, and why?** This question is particularly useful as a feedback dialogue starter when assignments are substantial, such as long reports or dissertations. Students quite often know exactly where they were trying to firm up an idea, but struggling to express it. Their help in bringing to our attention the exact positions of such instances can save us hours in finding them, and can ensure that we have the opportunity to respond helpfully and relevantly to students' needs.

39

Further questions to elicit reflection

Questions that aid deep reflection are rarely single questions, but tend to form clusters. There is often a starter question that sets the agenda, and frequently it is a 'what?' question. Then come the more important ones – the 'how?' questions and the 'why?' questions – and sometimes the '. . . else?' questions that ask for even deeper thinking and reflection.

In general, simple 'yes/no' questions can rarely make possible the extent of reflection that can be prompted by more open-ended questions such as 'to what extent . . .?'. Sadly, however, there remain far too many 'closed' questions on student feedback questionnaires, and, unsurprisingly, the level of student reflection that such questionnaires tend to elicit is limited.

There follow some clusters of questions, this time written with 'I' referring to the person self-assessing. The first part tends to be a scene-setting starter, and the sub-questions that follow are probing or clarifying questions intentionally leading towards deeper or more focused reflection. These questions are not in any particular order. A set of questions to aid student reflection on a piece of work just finished could use some of these as starting points and usefully add in subject-specific questions to help to flesh out the agenda for reflection.

Although these questions have been written with student reflection in mind, they could equally be extended to continuing professional development contexts, appraisal contexts, and suggesting some agenda items for a teaching portfolio for lecturers. Whatever the context, however, the quality of reflection that is prompted is only as good as the questions that prompt it. In other words, for optimum reflection, much more care needs to be taken with phrasing the questions than might have been thought necessary. Or, to put it more bluntly, when students seem to have difficulty in evidencing their reflection on their learning, it is often the case that we haven't yet spent nearly sufficient time on setting up the contexts in which we ask them to reflect.

1 **What did I actually achieve with this piece of work?** Which were the most difficult parts, and why were they difficult for me? Which were the most straightforward parts, and why did I find these easy?

2   **How well do I think I achieved the intended learning outcomes for this task?** Where could I have improved my achievement? Why didn't I improve it at the time?

3   **What have I got out of doing this assignment?** How have I developed my knowledge and skills? How do I see the pay-off from doing this assignment helping me in the longer term?

4   **What *else* have I got out of doing this assignment?** Have I developed other skills and knowledge that may be useful elsewhere at another time? If so, what are my own *emergent* learning outcomes from doing this assignment?

5   **What was the best thing I did?** Why was this the best thing I did? How do I know that this was the best thing I did?

6   **What worked least well for me?** Why did this not work well for me? What have I learned about the topic concerned from this not having worked well for me? What have I learned about myself from this not having worked well for me? What do I plan to do differently in future as a result of my answers to the above questions?

7   **With hindsight, how would I go about this assignment differently if I were doing it again from scratch?** To what extent will this assignment influence the way I tackle anything similar in future?

8   **What did I find the greatest challenge in doing this work?** Why was this a challenge to me? To what extent do I feel I have met this challenge? What can I do to improve my performance when next meeting this particular sort of challenge?

9   **What, for me, was the most boring or tedious part of doing this assignment?** Can I see the point of doing these things? If not, how could the assignment have been redesigned to make it more stimulating and interesting for me?

10   **Has it been worth the effort I put in?** Do the marks represent a just reward? Should this assignment be worth more or fewer marks in the overall scheme of things?

11   **Do I feel that my time on this assignment has been well spent?** If not, how could I have used my time more sensibly? Or should the assignment have been designed differently? Which parts of the assignment represent the time best spent? Which parts could be thought of as time wasted?

12   **How useful do I expect the feedback that I receive on my efforts for this assignment to be?** What sorts of feedback do I really want at present? What sorts of feedback do I really *need* at present? What are my expectations of getting useful feedback now, based on the feedback (or lack of it) that I've already received on past work?

13   **Overall, how has this assignment helped (or hindered) my motivation to learn more about this part of my syllabus?** Has it encouraged me, or disillusioned me?

14   **To what extent has this assignment helped me to clarify what I need to learn about this topic?** Have I a clearer picture after doing the assignment, or a foggier one? Who can help me gain a clearer picture, if the latter?

15   **To what extent has this assignment helped me to see where the goalposts stand for future assessments such as exams?** Has it given me useful insights into what will be expected of me in future?

16   **What advice would I give to a friend about to start on the same assignment?** How much time would I suggest that it would be worth putting into it? What pitfalls would I advise to be well worth not falling into?

17   **What are the three most important things that I think I need to do with this topic at this moment in time?** Which of these do I think is the most urgent for me to do? When will I aim to start doing this, and what is a sensible deadline for me to have completed it by?

40

Yet more questions to promote reflection

The following questions could be considered a starting point for reflection prompts to be included as leading questions for student self-assessment or student–tutor dialogues. Imagine that each time students handed in an assignment for marking (essay, report, problems-sheet solutions), or undertook any other assessed task (dissertation, fieldwork report, presentation), they were asked to reflect upon what they had just done, and show evidence of their reflection by answering some well-chosen questions about how they felt at that time about what they'd done. These questions could be conveniently spaced out on a pro forma of no more than two sides of A4, or the equivalent on a Web-based questionnaire.

Clearly, the number of questions used would need to be limited to (say) at most ten per assignment, and it would be appropriate to use different ones for each assignment, so that students did not just go into 'surface' mode when thinking about the questions. We have numbered the questions simply to help groups to discuss particular ones more easily than would be possible with a bullet-point list – the order of the questions is not significant here.

Finally, these questions are only intended to be illustrative. We hope they will help you to think of alternative questions that will be more relevant to the particular contexts of your own students' assessed work.

1 Which part of the assignment did you enjoy most?

2 How easy did you find it to use the resources?

3 How did you feel when you did this assignment?

4 Did you feel adequately prepared for this assignment?

5 Which type of learning technology did you find least relevant?

6 Did you have enough time to do this assignment? If not, why not?

7 How would you balance the marks for each section to reflect your effort?

8 What held you up more than anything else while working on this assignment?

9 Give a key moment when your understanding changed.

10 How relevant was this assignment to your workplace/course/life?

11 Was the level appropriate?

12 How has your learning on this task affected your practice?

13 How well do you think you referenced your work?

14 What, as a result of this work, have you learned that will help you in future assignments?

15 What would you most have liked to be assessed on?

16 What questions would you have liked to answer?

17 If you now had more time, what would you do next?

18 What new skill did you learn or develop through doing this?

19 What additional info would you seek out if you were doing it again?

20 What did you do that was innovative?

21 What risks did you take?

22 What surprised you that you learned from doing this assignment?

23 What one thing helped you (or would have helped you) to get started on this assignment?

24 What was your best work avoidance strategy before starting this assignment?

25 When did you start the assignment?

26 How relevant did you find this assignment?

27 Do you think that this is an improvement on your last assignment? Where? How?

28 Do you think the time spent on this was appropriate, considering its weighting in the module?

29 How clear did you find the assessment criteria for this assignment?

30 What other pieces of coursework were competing for your time while you were doing this assignment?

31 What's the best page? Why do you think this is the best page?

Chapter 6

Assessing group learning

41 Take the simplest path
42 Divide and concur
43 Add differentials
44 Add contribution marks
45 Add more tasks
46 Test them orally
47 Test them in writing

Assessing group learning is one of the most difficult tasks to do well. This is at least partly because there are two dimensions to group work, either or both of which may be involved in assessment: the product of the group work, and the processes that contributed to its development. However, the most important single issue is often the tricky matter of establishing the levels of contribution of respective members to both product and process alike.

There are several approaches to the task, each with its advantages and disadvantages. There is probably no single ideal way to assess group learning, and you will need to determine, in the context of your own work, the balance of the pros and cons of each of the approaches outlined in what follows.

Rather than present a series of tips on this complex topic, we give various overlapping possibilities, each with a number of pros and cons, adapted from Phil Race, *500 Tips on Group Learning* (Phil Race, London, Kogan Page, 2000) and based on *Strategies for Diversifying Assessment* (Brown, Rust and Gibbs, 1994). Notice that even in a given context the pros and cons listed can conflict with each other – groups can behave in very different ways.

41

Take the simplest path

The simplest path is just to use the same group mark for all involved.

Table 32 Group learning: advantages and disadvantages of giving all group members the same mark

Advantages	Disadvantages
• This approach is easy to manage. It is the least time-consuming of all the options available. • When group members know in advance that they will all receive equal credit for their work, they may be more willing to try to ensure for themselves that their contribution is equal. • It is worth considering if it is primarily the product of the group learning that is to be assessed, and not the processes leading up to this product. • It is useful if the assessment doesn't contribute to summative assessment, and learners are unlikely to be too concerned at their respective contributions to the work of the group not being assessed. • It can be appropriate if the task is fairly small, and it is felt that it would not be worth the time it would take to assess process as well as product. • Giving the same group mark is appropriate if the members of the group work well together and are in small, cohesive groups.	• Giving the same mark for all can be perceived as unfair, encouraging passengers, giving no bonus for excellence. • This approach does not acknowledge the importance of group processes, and therefore learners may not try to engage in the processes as seriously as they do when they know that process will count alongside product. • Groups may allow passengers on the first occasion this approach is used, but become resentful of them in future assessed group tasks, leading to dysfunctional groups later.

42

Divide and concur

Alternatively, you could divide up the assessed group task and assess each component separately.

Table 33 Group learning: advantages and disadvantages of dividing up the group task and assessing each component separately

Advantages	Disadvantages
• This can help groups to avoid disagreement, as everyone knows that their assessment will depend primarily on their own work. • This approach enables individuals to shine, and to know that the success of their work will be attributed directly to them. • This can work well when it is intended to assess group product rather than process, and when it is relatively easy to divide the product into separate, equal components. • This approach can be a way of ensuring that everyone shares the work of the group, each doing his or her own part of it. • Each member of the group carries responsibility for his or her own part of the overall work.	• It can be difficult to find equivalent tasks for all, and disputes may break out if some members of the group feel that they have been burdened with more demanding tasks than others. • The overall assessment load is increased, and it can be difficult to balance assessment decisions across the group, particularly if some members were set more demanding tasks than others. • Splitting up the work of the group goes against promoting interaction, and group processes may be regarded by group members as not being important. • Problems can arise when individuals don't pull their weight, and where passengers hinder other members of the group from developing their own elements of group product.

43

Add differentials

Another approach is to give a mark for the overall group product, but negotiate differentials between group members. For example, in a group of four members, award the group product 65 per cent, then ask the group to divide up (4 × 65 per cent) according to the way they feel the work was shared. You may need to decide whether to leave the differentials entirely to the group, or to make a ruling (for example) that a maximum differential should be 20 per cent.

Table 34 Group learning: advantages and disadvantages of negotiating differentials between group members

Advantages	Disadvantages
• This approach is perceived to be fair, and to place value on individual contribution to the work of the group. • This approach gives ownership to the group of the method of differentiation of the assessment of their overall work. • It is a method of assessing process as well as product, and causing the members of the group to reflect on their level of contribution to the overall product of the group. • When group members know that their contribution is going to be assessed, they may be more willing to set out to contribute fully to the work of the group. • The onus of awarding credit for group processes is taken away from the assessor, who may not in any case be in a good position to estimate the equivalence of contribution of members of the group.	• This approach needs a mature group to achieve consensus, and can be found very intimidating by groups whose members don't know each other very well. • This approach can result in everyone just agreeing to have the same mark, while causing internal resentments to build up inside the groups where contributions have not been equivalent, destabilising the group in future collaborative work together. • There can be substantial variations between groups in the ways they handle the task of distributing the credit for the products of their work, with some groups just making minor adjustments to the overall score, and other groups giving zero for a passenger and splitting up the remaining marks between the members who claim to have done the work.

Table 34 continued

Advantages	Disadvantages
	• If a particular score hovers close to an important borderline (such as that between an award of 'credit' or 'distinction', or a degree classification boundary), there could be the temptation to employ the differentials strategically to get as many members of the group as possible about particular borderlines, possibly at the expense of one member's award.

44

Add contribution marks

You could award a mark for the product of the group, and ask group members to peer-assess an additional mark for their contribution. In other words, for example, award each member of the group 65 marks for the product, and ask them to award each other member of the group between 0 and 10 for the extent to which they contributed to the work.

Table 35 Group learning: advantages and disadvantages of having group members peer-assess individual members' contributions

Advantages	Disadvantages
• This approach enables group members to feel that justice is being sought in the assessment of their work. • It encourages them to value process as well as outcome, and gives the message that process is regarded as being important. • The group members themselves may be the only people who can, if they are willing to do so, make a realistic assessment of each other's contributions to their overall work. • It can promote positive group behaviour, when group members are aware in advance that everyone in the group will be making an assessment of contribution to the work of the group. • A great deal of learning about process can be engendered by involving learners in well-organised peer assessment.	• Learners may turn round and say, 'It's your job, not mine, to assess my work.' • Training and practice are needed before group members enter into peer assessment, as they may be reluctant to mark down peers, and may agree to award each other equal (or maximum) marks for the process component of their work. • It takes careful organisation to get each member to record peer assessment scores for their colleagues, for example by secret ballot. • Members of some groups may be quite unwilling to make this kind of internal peer assessment, and may find it threatening to the bonding that may have developed during the group work.

45

Add more tasks

Alternatively, award an equal mark to each member for the product of the group task, then add individual assessed tasks for each member of the group.

Table 36 Group learning: advantages and disadvantages of adding individual assessed tasks

Advantages	Disadvantages
• This can be a way to accommodate the diversity of group members, and can allow them to take responsibility for allocating the additional tasks between group members. • It minimises the amount passengers can benefit. • It can offer scope for individuals to shine, and to get full credit for their individual strengths as demonstrated through the products of their separate tasks.	• This can make considerably more work for assessors. • Deciding on equivalent additional tasks can be difficult. • A group that plays to its strengths in the additional tasks will receive more credit than one that plays to its weaknesses. However, the learning pay-off will be better when groups decide to play to weaknesses, so the danger amounts to penalising groups that decide to go for high learning pay-off. • Reverting to individual work after group work may be seen by group members to undermine the perceived value of their group processes.

46

Test them orally

Consider awarding all group members the same mark for their product, but adding an individual viva (oral exam).

Table 37 Group learning: advantages and disadvantages of testing group members orally

Advantages	Disadvantages
• This enables assessors to test individual participation. Whether the viva is done with the group as a whole or with individual members separately, it is usually fairly easy to establish a reasonably accurate impression of whether the group members contributed equally to the work of the group.	• Vivas can be stressful. Some group members may not give an accurate impression of their contribution, either by (through shyness or modesty) underplaying their contribution, or by some members being able to 'fake good' in the viva when in fact their contribution was not good.
• The approach enables an element of differentiation, allowing the group members who may have done more than their share of the work to be rewarded.	• This approach makes more work for assessors.
• It is seen to be fair by group members, and if they know that this external check on their processes will take place in due course, they may be more willing to seek to contribute equally to the work.	• Subsequent groups (or group members) may have an unfair advantage if the questions used at the viva 'leak out' during the round of vivas, allowing them to rehearse their replies to the questions.
• Group members will be more willing to revisit what they did as a group, and to revise what they learned from the process, when they know that they could be asked to explain it again in the context of a viva.	• To be fair, the same questions need to be asked of each group (or each group member), but the best questions to use usually emerge gradually over a series of vivas.

47

Test them in writing

Alternatively, allow the group mark for the product to stand, but add a separate related assessment component to an exam.

Table 38 Group learning: advantages and disadvantages of testing group members in writing

Advantages	Disadvantages
• This approach makes it more difficult for most passengers to evade justice, and is perceived to be fair. • It can allow the most deserving individuals the opportunity to shine. • Knowing that group work remains on the exam agenda causes learners to include such work in their revision for exams, causing them to deepen their own learning by reflecting further on the group work.	• The exam may not be testing the same kinds of skills as the group work itself, and may unduly reward candidates who happen to be skilled at written exams. • More marking will be involved. • Some candidates are able to 'fake good' in written answers relating to the group work, even though they may not have contributed well to the work.

References and further reading

Allison, B and Race, P (2004) *The Student's Guide to Preparing Dissertations and Theses* London, Routledge.

Barnes, R (1995) *Successful Study for Degrees* London, Routledge.

Bates, A W (1995) *Technology, Open Learning and Distance Education* London, RoutledgeFalmer.

Baume, D (2001) *A Briefing on Assessment of Portfolios* Assessment Series no. 6, York, Learning and Teaching Support Network Generic Centre.

Beaty, L (1997) *Developing your Teaching through Reflective Practice* SEDA Special no. 5, Birmingham, SEDA Publications.

Bell, J (1999) *Doing your Research Project* Buckingham, UK, Open University Press.

Biggs, J (2003) *Teaching for Quality Learning at University* Buckingham, UK, Open University Press/SRHE.

Bligh, D (2000) *What's the Point in Discussion?* Exeter, UK, and Portland, Oregon, Intellect.

Bligh, D (2002) (6th edition) *What's the Use of Lectures?* San Francisco, Jossey-Bass.

Boud, D (1995) *Enhancing Learning through Self-Assessment* London, RoutledgeFalmer.

Brown, G (2001) *Assessment: A Guide for Lecturers* Assessment Series no. 3, York, Learning and Teaching Support Network Generic Centre.

Brown, G and Atkins, M (1988) *Effective Teaching in Higher Education* London, RoutledgeFalmer.

Brown, G with Bull, J and Pendlebury, M (1997) *Assessing Student Learning in Higher Education* London, RoutledgeFalmer.

Brown, S and Glasner, A (ed.) (1999) *Assessment Matters in Higher Education: Choosing and Using Diverse Approaches* Buckingham, UK, Open University Press.

Brown, S and Knight P (1994) *Assessing Learners in Higher Education* London: Kogan Page.

Brown, S and Race, P (2002) *Lecturing: A Practical Guide* London, RoutledgeFalmer.

Brown, S, Race, P and Bull, J (eds) (1999) *Computer Assisted Assessment in Higher Education* London, RoutledgeFalmer.

Brown, S, Rust, C and Gibbs, G (1994) *Strategies for Diversifying Assessment in Higher Education* Oxford, Oxford Centre for Staff Development.

Brown, S and Smith, B (July 1997) SEDA Special no. 3 *Getting to Grips with Assessment* Birmingham, SEDA Publications.

Chambers, E and Northedge, A (1997) *The Arts Good Study Guide* Milton Keynes, UK, Open University Worldwide.

Cowan, J (1998) *On Becoming an Innovative University Teacher: Reflection in Action* Buckingham, UK, Open University Press.

Creme, P and Lea, M R (2003) (2nd edition) *Writing at University: A Guide for Students* Buckingham, UK, Open University Press.

Cryer, P (2000) *The Research Student's Guide to Success* Buckingham, UK, Open University Press.

Daniel, J S (1996) *Mega-Universities and Knowledge Media: Technology Strategies for Higher Education* London, RoutledgeFalmer.

Evans, L and Abbott, I (1998) *Teaching and Learning in Higher Education* London, Cassell.

Fairbairn, G J and Winch, C (1996) (2nd edition) *Reading, Writing and Reasoning: A Guide for Students* Buckingham, UK, Open University Press.

Fry, H, Ketteridge, S and Marshall, S (2003) *A Handbook for Teaching and Learning in Higher Education: Enhancing Academic Practice* London, RoutledgeFalmer.

Gibbs, G (1992) *Assessing More Students* Oxford Centre for Staff Development, Oxford Brookes University, UK

Gibbs, G (1999) 'Using assessment strategically to change the way students learn', in S Brown and A Glasner (eds) *Assessment Matters in Higher Education: Choosing and Using Diverse Approaches*, A, Open University Press, Buckingham, UK.

Gray, D (2001) *A Briefing on Work-Based Learning* Assessment Series no. 11, York, Learning and Teaching Support Network Generic Centre.

Knight, P (ed.) (1995) *Assessment for Learning in Higher Education* SEDA Series, London, Kogan Page.

Knight, P (2001) *A Briefing on Key Concepts: Formative and Summative, Criterion and Norm-referenced Assessment* Assessment Series no. 7, York, Learning and Teaching Support Network Generic Centre.

Laurillard, D (2001) *Rethinking University Teaching* London, RoutledgeFalmer.

McCarthy, D and Hurst, A (2001) *A Briefing on Assessing Disabled Students* Assessment Series no. 8, York, Learning and Teaching Support Network Generic Centre.

Mortiboys, A (March 2002) *The Emotionally Intelligent Lecturer* SEDA Special no .12, Birmingham, SEDA Publications.

Murphy, R (2001) *A Briefing on Key Skills in Higher Education* Assessment Series no. 5, York, Learning and Teaching Support Network Generic Centre.

Mutch, A and Brown, G (2001) *Assessment: A Guide for Heads of Department* Assessment Series no. 2, York, Learning and Teaching Support Network Generic Centre.

Northedge, A (2004) *The Good Study Guide* Milton Keynes, UK, Open University Worldwide.

Northedge, A, Thomas, J, Lane, A and Peasgood, A (1997) *The Sciences Good Study Guide* Milton Keynes, UK, Open University Worldwide.

Race, P (1999) *How to Get a Good Degree* Buckingham, UK, Open University Press.

Race, P (ed.) (1999) *2000 Tips for Lecturers* London, RoutledgeFalmer,

Race, P (2000) *How to Win as a Final-Year Student* Buckingham, UK, Open University Press.

Race, P (2001a) *A Briefing on Self, Peer and Group Assessment* Assessment Series no. 9, York, Learning and Teaching Support Network Generic Centre.

Race, P (2001b) *Assessment: A Guide for Students* Assessment Series no. 4, York, Learning and Teaching Support Network Generic Centre.

Race, P (2001c) (2nd edition) *The Lecturer's Toolkit* London, RoutledgeFalmer.

Race, P (2003) *How to Study: Practical Tips for Students* Oxford, Blackwell.

Race P and Brown S (2004) (2nd edition) *500 Tips for Tutors* London, RoutledgeFalmer.

Ramsden, P (1992) *Learning to Teach in Higher Education* London, RoutledgeFalmer.

Rowntree, D (1989) (2nd revised edition) *Assessing Students: How Shall we Know Them?* London, RoutledgeFalmer.

Rust, C (2001) *A Briefing on Assessment of Large Groups* Assessment Series no. 12, York, Learning and Teaching Support Network Generic Centre.

Schwartz, P and Webb, G (eds) (2002) *Assessment: Case Studies, Experience and Practice from Higher Education* London, RoutledgeFalmer.

Stefani, L and Carroll, J (2001) *A Briefing on Plagiarism* Assessment Series no. 10, York, Learning and Teaching Support Network Generic Centre.

Tracy, E (2002) *The Student's Guide to Exam Success* Buckingham, UK, Open University Press.

Yorke, M (2001) *Assessment: A Guide for Senior Managers* Assessment Series no. 1, York, Learning and Teaching Support Network Generic Centre.

Index

added value, self-assessment 146
administrating, peer assessment 140–3
administrative staff 111
agendas: peer assessment 139;
    self-evaluation 147–9
artefacts, peer assessment 134
articulacy 105–6
assignment return sheets 111, 115–16
audiences: presentations 87; reviews 61
audio tapes: feedback 108–9;
    performances 87; portfolios 73
authenticity 3; performances 86; portfolios
    71–2
averaging, peer assessment 140

benchmarking 2
bias, dissertations 98–9
bibliographies:
annotated 60–3
peer assessment 133–4
brainstorming: essays 59; exam questions
    36; peer assessment 137
budgets: feedback 108; poster displays 96;
    unseen exams 27
burden reduction 111–12

calculations 23, 133, 136
case-study information 30
cheating 16–17
class exercises, exam questions 36–7
classification: of students 6; system 7
class lists 110
class reports 116–17
codes 107, 109, 117–18

collaboration 16–17; poster displays 95;
    reports 64, 65–6; reviews 62, 63
colleagues 19; exam questions 29;
    inspection process 43; marking
    schemes 32; multiple choice exams 48;
    in other universities 19; portfolios 74;
    vivas 50–1; work-based learning 100
competition: performances 87;
    presentations 81–5
computer-adaptive testing 54
computer-based self-assessment 145
computer-delivered feedback 124–5
computer-generated feedback 128–9
computer-mediated coursework 125
computers: conferences 123–4, 127–8;
    electronic feedback 122–9; email
    feedback 109, 122–3, 125–8, 129;
    feedback records 110; laboratory
    reports 66; multiple choice
    marking 48; progress monitoring 99;
    word-processed comments 114;
    word-processed overall class reports
    116–17
conferences, computer 123–4, 127–8
consequential marks 32
consistency, performances 86
constructive alignment 12
context-specific assessment 9
continuous methodology 9
contribution marks 161
convergent assessment 9
copying 16–17
creativity, portfolios 74
criterion referencing 9

cultural differences 17
cumulative methodology 9

deadlines 11; excuses 21–2; reports 66; student projects 91
debriefing 117–18; poster displays 94; vivas 51
deep learning 3, 9, 132
diagnostic assessment 10
differentials, group learning 159–60
dissertations 97–9; binding 99; past examples 98
distractors, multiple choice 46, 47
divergent assessment 9
drafts: feedback 24; marking schemes 32

editing, peer assessment 138
efficiency 4
electronic feedback 122–9
email, feedback 109, 122–3, 125–8, 129
empowerment, feedback 106
end point methodology 9
equity 3, 86
essays 56–9; plans, peer assessment 133; word limit 22
exams 26–54; computer-adaptive testing 54; failure coping 37–9; in-tray 53–4; multiple-choice 44–8, 54; objective structured clinical 53; open-book 40–1; open-notes 42–3; oral 49–52, 99, 163; peer assessment 143; practical work 67; structured 44–8; student difficulties 22; take-away 54; technique 38; timed 27–39, 46; what not to do 22; what they measure 34–5
exhibitions 74, 93–6, 134
external assessors 19–20

face-to-face feedback 119–21
fairness 3, 17; self-evaluation 148; unseen exams 27–8; vivas 49
feedback 18–19, 104–29; electronic 122–9; essays 59; face-to-face 119–21; from colleagues 29; help maximization 107–9; multiple choice exams 46, 47; portfolios 73, 74; presentations 85; reflective questions 152; reports 66; student exam report 33–4; student projects 91; support levels 24; teaching

faults 6; unseen exams 27–8, 33–4; vivas 51; word use 106; written or print 22, 113–18, 126
flexible learning 145
format: portfolios 72; reports 65
formative assessment 3–4, 5, 9, 11

global feedback 105, 126
grades 108
group learning 156–64; contribution marks 161; differentials 159–60; divide and concur 158; individual assessment tasks 162; oral testing 163; presentations competition 81–5; self assessment 145; simplest path 157; teamwork 8; written tests 164
guessing, multiple choice 44, 47

halo effects 33, 57
handouts, poster displays 94
hard-copy feedback 113–18
holistic assessment 9
honesty 108

identity of students 21
incremental assessment 4
inspection process 43
inter-assessor reliability 2
interim assessment, portfolios 73
Internet: computer-delivered feedback 124; exam questions 37; reflective questions 153; self-assessment 145
interviews, peer assessment 133
intra-assessor reliability 2
in-tray exams 53–4
ipsative assessment 9

journals: self-assessment 144; work-based learning 102

knowledge: application 8; vs regurgitation 8

laboratory reports 66
layout, unseen exams 30
learning 3; contracts 146; deep 3, 9, 132; flexible 145; prior 145; strategic 9; surface 9, 28; work-based 100–3
learning outcomes: alignment 7; design

12–15; linking 12–15; portfolios 72; posters 93; in practice 7; question drafting 29; reflective questions 151; student projects 90; transparency 2; unseen exams 30–1
legibility 107
library staff 62, 91
licence to practise 7
linking: learning outcomes 12–15; posters 95

marking schemes: design 31–2; essays 58; multiple choice 47; overloaded 112; student version 37
mentors 102
model answers 31, 36, 107–8, 114–15
monitoring, peer assessment 136
mood changes 33
motivation: comments 107; learning 3; reflective questions 152
multiple choice exams 44–8, 54

norm referencing 9
notes, keeping 19

objective structured clinical exams (OSCEs) 53
on-demand exams 48
open-book exams 40–1
open days 95
open-notes exams 42–3
optical mark-reading 48
options choice 5, 6, 39
oral exams 49–52, 99, 163
overview of marking 18
ownership: learning outcomes 13; peer assessment 132, 140; portfolios 72

parallel marking 135
peer assessment 111, 131–43; criteria formulation 137–43; essays 59; grids 142–3; performances 87; poster displays 93, 94, 95; practical work 70; presentations 80; reports 66; self-assessment preparation 145; starting 135–6; student projects 91
peer comparisons 7
performances 86–8, 134
piloting, marking schemes 32

plagiarism 16–17
portfolios 71–7; peer assessment 134; self-evaluation 146; student projects 91; work-based learning 102
poster displays 93–6; past examples 96; peer assessment 134
Post-it™ notes: dissertations 99; exams 33; feedback 107; portfolios 73; self-evaluation 144; vivas 50
practical work 66–7, 68–70, 134
practice: exam simulation 38; multiple choice 47; peer assessment 135; poster displays 95; presentations 79–80; vivas 50, 52
prejudices 33
presentations 78–85, 133
prioritising, peer assessment 138
prior learning 145
pro formas: assignment return sheets 111, 115–16; exams 33; portfolios 73, 75–7; reflective questions 153; reports 66; self-evaluation 147; vivas 51
projects 89–92; design 90–2; past examples 91
proof-reading 31

Quality Assurance Agency 18
quality monitoring 18–20
question banks 48

records, feedback 110–11
redemption of failure 4
reflective questions 150–5
reliability 2; multiple choice 44; work-based learning 100
reports 64–7, 133
reviews 60–3
revision plans 38
ripples on a pond model 12, 13
role-play, vivas 52

second markers 33
self-assessment 3, 111, 131, 144–9; learning outcomes 15; performances 87; portfolios 74; practical work 70; student projects 92; tutor dialogues 147–9
self-esteem 38
serialistic assessment 9

sharing, peer assessment 138
special needs 18, 21, 45
spell checking 127
staggered assessment 95
standards: excellence 4; learning
    outcomes 14; practical work 69;
    reliability 2; setting 6; unseen exams 30;
    upward-creeping 19
statement banks 111
statistics 7, 128
strategic learning 9
stress, presentations 88
structured exams 44–8
subjectivity: performances 86; posters 93;
    theses 97
sudden death syndrome 4
summative assessment 3, 9
supplementary questions 70
support: dissertations 98; self-assessment
    145
surface learning 9, 28

take-away exams 54
targets, progressive 112
theses 97–9
time: peer assessment 136; projects 91;
    unseen exams 30

timed exams 27–39, 46
timing: of assessment 4, 9, 10–11, 21, 69;
    feedback 105
topic menu 43
transparency 2, 131
tutor dialogues 147–9

unseen exams 27–39

validity 2; bibliographies 60; essays 56;
    in-tray exams 54; multiple choice 44;
    open-book exams 40; performances 86;
    portfolios 71; take-away exams 54;
    unseen exams 27
venue: presentations 80; vivas 50
video tapes: performances 87; portfolios
    73; posters 96; presentations 79, 80;
    self-assessment 146; vivas 52
vivas 49–52, 99, 163

weighting criteria 24; peer assessment 139;
    posters 96; presentations 79
word limits 22, 58, 62, 111
work-based learning 100–3
work load reduction 110–12
work logs 102
written comments 22, 113–18, 126